PROSPERITY WITH A PURPOSE

Christian Faith and Values in a Time of Rapid Economic Growth

IRISH CATHOLIC BISHOPS' CONFERENCE

VERITAS

First published 1999 by
Veritas Publications
7/8 Lower Abbey Street
Dublin 1

Copyright © Irish Catholic Bishops' Conference, 1999

ISBN 1 85390 349 3

Designed by Bill Bolger
Printed in the Republic of Ireland by Betaprint Ltd, Dubli

CONTENTS

PART ONE

Introduction

1.0 *Why we write*

1. The last years of the twentieth century have added an exceptional dimension to the transition to a new millennium in Ireland. The economy of the Republic of Ireland has undergone a singular transformation; it has surmounted crippling weaknesses to attract widespread recognition for its impressive performance.[1] No part of the island and no individual on it has been wholly insulated from the effects of this turnaround.

2. This transformation invites careful appraisal. There is much to be thankful for, and much of which to be proud. At the same time, the economic boom has brought new and urgent demands. Soaring house prices, congested roads and an acute shortage of childcare facilities have been the most dramatic evidence that the Irish economy has rapidly outgrown the framework that housed it. The preparation of the Republic's National Development Plan for the years 2000-2006 brought attention to the scale of the investments needed to push back the different constraints on the economy's potential for further growth.

3. This Letter invites reflection on a different set of demands. These too are urgent, not in order to keep the economy growing but because meeting them helps ensure there is moral purpose to Ireland's new prosperity. Demands of this kind could be neglected without economic growth being choked off but, if they are overlooked, huge opportunities for the enrichment of people's lives will be lost. These demands are moral challenges on one of two levels: some require a response from Ireland's social institutions and political system and are, therefore, addressed primarily to Government and the social partners; others are addressed to each and every one of us as individuals.

4. Ireland enters the twenty-first century with unique opportunities for redressing fundamental problems that have beset its society for a very long time. The performance of the Irish economy during the last decade of the twentieth century has been described as 'peerless'.[2] Irish people should now be determined that future commentators will have cause to speak of equally impressive social achievements on the island during the first decade of the new century. These years will, in all probability, present unprecedented opportunities: to reduce poverty and educational disadvantage from among the highest to among the lowest levels in the EU; to ensure no child is reared in poverty; to end extreme social segregation in the Irish pattern of housing; to adopt best practice in every area of care for the island's environment; to become an increasingly credible and effective advocate of the cause of the poorest nations.

5. Such objectives are not unbridled idealism; high social objectives and their attainment are the least the current situation requires. It was an Ireland apparently saddled with an endemic labour surplus, chronic public debt and unjust distribution of taxation that achieved the major economic turnaround. The stronger Ireland of today should not set narrow boundaries to what it can yet do for those of its people who remain poor, unemployed or otherwise socially disadvantaged.

6. Christians, with the understanding of the human person and society that their faith gives them, are called to play a full part as their society sets its social objectives and debates the strategies for attaining them.

7. The economic achievements of the 1990s required more than foreign capital and favourable international circumstances. Significant inputs of solidarity, intelligence, hard work and innovative ability were also needed. It might be thought that the economic success recorded would only further strengthen such values in Irish life so that the country can press on all the more easily to complete its unfinished social business. But the link between economic growth and the political will and social values that ensure social progress is not so convenient.

8. Many people are experiencing growing difficulties in maintaining the balance they want in their lives between their family and their work, their standard of living and compassion for people less fortunate than they are, their lifestyle and the place of social and community involvement in it. The economic boom of the 1990s has, indeed, given many people significantly more purchasing power yet, at every level, there are those who feel under increasing pressure. The expanding economy is imposing frequent changes on them, and intensifying competition is raising the penalties for failure as well as the rewards for success. People at work, especially those who are also parents, have become particularly conscious of a shortage of time, of insecurities surrounding their current livelihood, and of the weight on them of others' expectations.

9. In some respects, it is becoming more difficult to give practical expression to spiritual values – to show that a job, while paid, is primarily about service of others, to protect the quality of time given to family and friends, to enjoy quiet and solitude, and to practise prayer and contemplation. Competitive pressures are also making it difficult to maintain involvement in voluntary and community issues, to appreciate the natural environment for itself and as a legacy to future generations, to develop a stronger sense of citizenship and responsibility for what is public, to nurture a concern for fairness and indignation at poverty, and to show pride that Ireland should contribute fully to a more just and peaceful world beyond its shores.

10. This Letter will argue that people need to foster more vigorously than ever their spiritual values precisely in order to ensure that genuine personal contentment and stronger family life will result from higher material standards of living. The presence of these values and their practical expression in Irish life is a type of 'capital' too, different to the physical and human capital of economic studies. It is a cultural and social capital that enables individuals to find purpose in earning and see meaning in taxation, that guides their consumption, and brings them to use extra wealth to widen and deepen their relationships with others. This capital too needs fresh

investment, in every decade and each generation. Otherwise, a widely treasured quality to life on this island will be found to have slipped away. It would be unthinkable that the Christian faith did not have a huge contribution to make in this area. For the Christian, greater control over economic resources is a challenge and an opportunity to forge wider, more respectful and more convivial human relationships; it should not be a blight on them.

11. Over the past fifteen hundred years, the history and culture of Ireland have been intertwined with Christian faith and living. The weeds that have also grown during this period have not prevented a rich harvest being reaped (Mt 13:24-31). Many who have lived on this island were helped by the Christian faith to make sense of their lives and live them in a deeply human way. In particular, a great number of people lived through times of oppression and acute hardship mindful of their dignity and resilient in finding solutions, helped by their relationship with Christ and communion with the Universal Church. This has been despite human frailty, institutional failure, and the different ways that historical and social forces have used the Christian message for their own purposes.

12. It is our conviction that the Christian message retains all its potential to enable people in Ireland to meet the novel challenges and opportunities of economic wealth in an authentically human way. We say this despite abuses that have been perpetrated by some trusted representatives of the Church. But while we wrestle with the implications of those shameful events, and the legacy of an Ireland in which people who were poor had few, if any, rights acknowledged, we know that the strength and power of the Christian Gospel are not, ultimately, dependent on weak human beings. Confidence in the Gospel, therefore, rather than in ourselves, brings us to hope that this Letter will be an encouragement to everyone concerned about the quality of individual and social life in Ireland. Its purpose is to give a Christian perspective on the unprecedented economic expansion that the country is experiencing.

13. This Letter is relevant to people in Northern Ireland too. There is a widespread appreciation that great mutual benefit can now be reaped through having stronger links and increased policy co-ordination between the economies of the two parts of Ireland. Though the economic boom in the Republic is this Letter's starting point, its central concerns are to strengthen the role of social and ethical values in economic life, and to do that by bringing the person and message of Jesus to address directly the preoccupations with earning, acquiring possessions and consuming which are so characteristic of current Western civilisation. The values and principles espoused here, therefore, are applicable to the pursuit of justice, solidarity and social love within each of the institutional and policy frameworks of Ireland, north and south.

14. Only strong spiritual and social values, with their practical embodiment in institutions and policies as well as expression in individual behaviour, will ensure that greater wealth improves the quality of life on this island in a true sense. In Christian social teaching, these values are a reminder that quality of life is inconceivable without quality of relationships. This teaching urges us to value greater economic wealth precisely because it offers new opportunities to deepen and widen the human relationships that fundamentally determine who we are. It is of failure to see this that the Gospels do their utmost to warn those who set their hearts on wealth: they 'win the world but lose themselves' (Mk 8:36; Lk 12:16-21 and 16:9-13). The full force of this extraordinary message is that the final victims of poverty in the midst of plenty are not those excluded from consumption, but those doing the consuming; selfishly appropriating what others have much greater need of diminishes the individual's own humanity. It is not a new message, nor a popular one in a world as divided as our own, but it is the Gospel message.

15. For this reason, to rescue the humanity of the rich as well as of the poor, the Christian message forcefully reminds every society that, if it would know the true answer to the question, 'Is greater wealth improving us as a people?', it should consult

the most vulnerable in its midst. The Old Testament prophets repeatedly looked to what was happening to the weak and defenceless ('the widow, the orphan and the stranger in your midst') to know if the people were being faithful to the pact God made when He entrusted the land to Israel. Similarly today, if Ireland wants to be sure that greater economic wealth is improving it as a people, it should seek to ensure that anyone who runs a high risk of being socially excluded should 'have cause to bless' its booming economy 'from their hearts' (Job 31:19). This means devising and implementing imaginative policies that benefit, for example, the person who is long-term unemployed, the homeless person, the child growing up in a low-income family, the person working long and awkward hours but still earning extremely little, the parent left to bring up children on her or his own, the vulnerable older person, the asylum-seeker, the Traveller, the person wrestling with an addiction to drugs, the prisoner, and the person with a disability.

16. Christian social teaching is enriched by the tradition of the Jubilee year in the Bible. The amnesties that characterised a Jubilee year – slaves were to be freed, debts cancelled, and property to revert to its original owners – served to remind the people that the land in which they lived belonged to God and had been received as a collective gift.[3] In recognition of that, individual ownership was never to mean selfish appropriation and exclusion, but the exercise by each of a stewardship that benefited both self and the community. The Great Jubilee of the year 2000, therefore, in Ireland or anywhere, is properly celebrated, not by the construction of grandiose public works, or in lavish public and private entertainments, but by giving new and practical expression to the radical equality that God has established between all human beings. In preparing this Letter, we were impressed by the number of people who expressed to us in different ways a concern that, for greater economic wealth to profit Irish society, spiritual values would not only need to be retained but deepened. This Letter will have done something to meet their concern and ours if it encourages more people to welcome the new millennium by

giving some specific expression to their desire to see economic activity genuinely enhance the quality of life for everyone.

17. This Letter is far from being a comprehensive or final word on the social and economic changes that Ireland is experiencing. With *The Work of Justice* (1977), *Christian Faith in a Time of Economic Depression* (1983), and *Work is the Key* (1992), it continues an ongoing Christian reflection on the nature, causes and potential of the changes Irish society is undergoing as the twenty-first century begins. In preparing it, we have endeavoured to consult widely, and were heartened and moved by the experience and expertise, the goodwill and expectations, the energy and lived example, of many and diverse people. They included workers and business leaders, people dependent on social welfare and senior civil servants, people active in voluntary organisations and academics. To all those who came to talk to us, who took part in discussion groups, who wrote to us briefly or at length, to the organisations and groups who forwarded submissions and background documentation, we are deeply grateful.

PART TWO

Looking Back

2.0 *Why look back?*

18. It is important to look back at the circumstances of Ireland's economic turnaround for three reasons. First, the scale of what happened during the 1990s needs to be kept alive in the public consciousness. Otherwise, the new problems that rapid economic growth brings with it will obscure people's collective memory and dissipate their sense of relief about what has been left behind.

19. Second, appreciating how the turnaround happened makes clear that the Republic of Ireland is being asked to deal, not with a temporary surge in its level of economic activity, but with a long-prepared, carefully founded, and sustainable change in its economy. It is true that economic growth rates cannot continue indefinitely at the high levels of the 1994-1999 period. But this must not be allowed to lessen Irish society's willingness to undergo a thorough revision of its attitudes and behaviour, its policies and institutions, needed **now** in order to address urgent challenges.

20. A third reason for looking back is to appreciate the role that social values have **already** played in the transformation of the 1990s. The valuable work of different inquiries exposes the absence of social values in the lives of individuals who took advantage of privileged positions to undermine the common good. But despite the greed of a few, the economic boom was bolstered by the restraint, co-operation and solidarity practised by the many during the 1990s. Irish society is by no means starting from scratch as it seeks inner strength to meet the challenges of the next decade. However, the current strength of social values in Irish life cannot be expected to survive let alone develop as the automatic result of past success. In particular, any fatigue in the spirit of partnership needs to be addressed, while any sense that buoyant economic conditions lessen one's own group's responsibility for the common good needs to be vigorously checked.

21. In the last six years of the twentieth century, the level of economic activity in the Irish economy (real GDP) increased by more than 60 per cent.[4] The significance of such a figure is not that it 'scored' well above what was happening in any other advanced industrial country, but that it reflected and confirmed that extraordinary changes were **again** taking place throughout Irish society. 'Again', because the effervescent 1960s also saw real GDP rise substantially (in fact, over the fourteen years, 1960-73, it increased by 70 per cent), and that period is remembered equally for the cultural and social changes that occurred as for its economic and employment growth rates.

22. The severe recession of the 1980s had coloured not just business outlooks and political programmes but economic forecasting and historical assessments. It is hard to identify any major group or organisation in the early 1990s that foresaw the scale of the transformation to come. In preparing *Work is the Key* (1992), a great deal of consultation and of listening to experts in many disciplines gave no inkling of the imminence of a major turnaround in the economy. The mood then was even reminiscent of the late 1950s, when observers wondered if the Irish State would ever succeed in housing a modern, self-sustaining economy. By contrast, the business outlooks and expert forecasts of late 1999 were strongly positive. It is clear that the economic boom had done an enormous amount to dispel pessimism and foster confidence.

23. Starting around 1993, the Irish economy not only shook off recession but resumed growth at a rate well above its long-term growth path. The real dynamism and wonder of the boom was on the employment front: from being an economy capable of generating considerable increases in wealth with relatively few extra workers, the Irish economy became hungry for human labour. The European Union had looked with some envy in the early 1990s at the impressive job creation of the US economy and been aware that Ireland was one of its

unemployment black spots. However, cumulative employment growth in Ireland outstripped that of the US and, between 1993 and 1998, was without parallel in the advanced industrialised world.[5] As a result, dangerous levels of public borrowing and chronically high unemployment and emigration in the late 1980s were replaced within ten years by healthy public finances and a business community busily hiring people and devising strategies to overcome shortages of workers. A fatalism in the early 1990s at the inevitability of high unemployment gave way by the end of the decade to confidence in the feasibility and eventuality of full employment.

2.2 *Appreciating the causes of the turnaround*

24. A lot of attention has deservedly been given to the causes of this extraordinary turnaround. Listing the factors most usually highlighted serves to make the point that the boom was broadly based; it certainly had no single cause.[6] The main factors highlighted are (without attempting to list them in order of importance): Ireland's well-educated young population; the ability of the Irish economy, once growing rapidly, to attract back former emigrants with skills and experience acquired abroad; the willingness to take employment of a large number of educated women who had hitherto remained in the home; the strength of the US economy and the attractiveness to many of its companies of Ireland as an English-speaking, foreign investor-friendly, low-cost business location within the Single European Market (particularly for the IT industry); the maturity and common purpose which the political parties and successive governments brought to managing the nation's finances; the unprecedented degree of consultation and co-operation practised by the social partners in the policy-formation process at national level; the contribution to the level and quality of public capital investment made by the EU's structural funds; the increased competition and rewards for good practice in the corporate sector (and punishment for bad) that came from the creation of the Single European Market; changes in the taxation and

social welfare codes that made it increasingly attractive to work at relatively low incomes.

25. In addition to this range of factors which mutually reinforced each other, commentators have also underlined the fortuitous element of timing as helping the economic boom; many international markets moved in directions that were particularly helpful to the Irish economy in the 1990s (with agriculture as the major exception). Lower international interest rates, favourable currency movements, an economic upswing in Europe, continuing strong growth in the US economy – none of these factors was within Irish control, but collectively they meant that policy improvements taking place in Ireland were doubly rewarded.

2.3 *Appreciating the role of values*

26. The economic transformation of the 1990s was not the product of exclusively economic ingredients. Key social and cultural values worked in and through the more frequently cited economic factors. It is important, as Irish society adjusts itself to higher employment rates and higher disposable incomes, that it not lose sight of the quality of human commitment that was also part of the transformation, and the evidence that the common good was a dominant consideration in the formation and implementation of policies at crucial moments.

27. For example, Ireland, in the 1990s, benefited considerably from a heightened level of **trust** among the main actors in its economy. This was accomplished principally through the series of national agreements that began with the Programme for National Recovery in 1987.[7] As experience in working together grew, the list of problems for which joint responsibility was accepted also lengthened. **Solidarity** with those marginalised by the processes of economic change began to figure on the agenda for successive national agreements, culminating in the actual inclusion of some of their representatives in the talks that produced Partnership 2000, the programme covering

1997-2000. Despite imbalances in their terms, and tensions in their interpretation, these agreements enabled the key actors in the economy to direct more energy to confronting common challenges together, rather than to trying to establish the superiority of their own perspectives. Individual actors felt they had a greater degree of security from being harmed by the unilateral action of another, and that there was a new channel of appeal and redress open to them. For these reasons, a period of major structural change that generated many opportunities for disagreement and conflict, particularly at the level of the individual enterprise, witnessed remarkable industrial and social peace. Of all the factors usually listed as helping to cause the economic boom, perhaps none has as high a moral content as the development of social partnership.

28. It can help to offset any exaggeration of what was achieved during the 1990s to appreciate that the part played by trust and other values was not so much because Ireland 're-wrote the rule book' governing economic growth and development but, more accurately, learned to read pages that had hitherto been neglected. There is wide evidence that economic prosperity is more easily attained – and maintained – by societies in which there is widespread trust, and a developed **civic culture**.[8] Church social teaching too has never supported the view that economic transactions take place in a moral-free zone. Rather, it emphasises the extent to which 'the fundamental and positive role of business, the market, private property and the resulting responsibility for the means of production, as well as free human creativity in the economic sector' presupposes and benefits from a strong, sheltering, institutional, juridical and political framework (*Centesimus Annus*: 42, 48).[9] Ireland travelled considerable distance during the 1990s in leaving behind assumptions that any group was above the law, beyond the obligations of transparency and disclosure, or so competent and capable as to be able to deliver on economic and social objectives on its own.

29. Social partnership during the opening years of the twenty-first century cannot be presumed on; it needs to be constantly

renewed. Its great contribution in the 1990s may quickly fade from the memories of those who were not then participants. Its institutional expression deserves continuing innovation. For example, there is a need to develop further the spirit and practice of partnership at company level, to strengthen the inclusion of the community and voluntary sector, and ensure the harmonisation of the national process with structures at the regional and local levels. Trading extensively in the Euro zone, the Single European Market and the global economy do not make unilateral action by any of Ireland's social partners potentially less damaging to society today; very much the contrary. Hard work, careful analysis, repeated consultation, patient negotiation, courageous leadership and, when necessary, institutional innovations characterised the national partnership process that helped to generate the turnaround in the Irish economy. The same qualities will help to make Ireland's stronger economy progressively more just, participatory and sustainable over the first decade of the twenty-first century.

30. Many people made their response to the crises of the late 1980s (in unemployment and the public finances) through the quality of their daily work; there they displayed their civic commitment, engendered trust and fostered partnership. In diverse areas, leadership, a priority to what will work rather than how things have 'always' been done, the embrace of systematic consultation, feedback and evaluation, and the study of best international practice, have produced more effective policies, with substantial positive benefits for society at large.

31. Some examples illustrate this new spirit in working. The collection of tax revenue has become enormously more effective; that twice the amount of revenue was collected in 1997 as in 1988 was not the effect of economic growth alone. Industrial policy has been the subject of successive evaluations and redesigns, making possible substantial new achievements; the acceleration in inward investment was the fruit of careful analysis as well as of favourable international developments.

Community-based responses to social disadvantage have grown in numbers and sophistication and, by the end of the 1990s, were winning accommodating changes in the structures and strategies of many statutory bodies. Some local authorities have developed integrated strategies for regenerating urban areas in close consultation with local residents. Links have steadily multiplied between Irish universities and the business world; these and other research initiatives are welcome pointers to how the knowledge-base to the country's new prosperity has begun to develop on the island itself. Several government departments have co-operated in introducing new schemes that give many unemployed people the concrete experience that taking a job or improving their skills brings tangible rewards from society, rather than making their lives more difficult. Of course, contrasting examples of poor-quality programmes, blocking bureaucracies, arrogant management and short-term expediency can also be given. However, they capture far less of what characterised the 1990s.[10]

32. Love of county and of country tends not to figure in conventional studies of the factors that cause rapid economic growth. It would be wrong, however, to dismiss its contribution in reversing Ireland's economic fortunes. The success story of the 1990s would not have been the same without such factors as former emigrants' attachment to Ireland and their willingness to return, the readiness of successful entrepreneurs and company executives overseas with Irish roots to begin investing in the country, the huge commitment of the religious orders and the Church to education, which gave generations of Irish young people standards far beyond what the State alone could have achieved, the element of loyalty that characterised many people's attachment to their place of work and led them to take pride and – when necessary – make sacrifices to enable their company or organisation win through to a better future. Particularly remarkable has been the huge amount of voluntary work done in organisations and communities around the country, and the profound sense of place associated with this that helped bring together people of different social classes and

professional backgrounds in the pursuit of local objectives. The main labour market programmes of the 1990s, designed to help unemployed people back into work, were, to a major extent, activated by community and voluntary organisations.

2.4 The economic boom as 'the work of many human hands'

33. In summary, it has often been *said* that people were Ireland's greatest resource, but the 1990s were the first decade in which the island's economic life effectively acknowledged that. The skill and effectiveness of the average person in employment continued to improve steadily[11] but, in a way unique in the history of the country since Independence, the proportions of the population resident in the State who were of age to work (15-64), who wanted to work (the participation rate), and who were able to find a job (none of which is the same thing), all grew together.[12] The boom is not expected to continue at the levels of the 1994-1999 period; there simply are not the same reserves of educated women in the home, skilled emigrants overseas and unemployed people in training upon whom to draw. However, a larger and more productive workforce and more numerous and better-managed companies are lasting achievements. They are solid grounds for believing that the Irish economy has definitively broken through to new and higher ground, and that its society should accordingly now seek to do so also.

34. It is true that individual material standards of living can increase faster when economic growth is driven primarily by raising productivity rather than by expanding employment. But the 'standard of living' surely means more to most Irish people than the goods and services their own household can enjoy. It also means a great deal to them that more people have stayed in the country and that less people are unemployed or discouraged from looking for a job. The huge reduction in unemployment, the massive cut in involuntary emigration, the ability of many former emigrants to return, the option open to more women of taking a job, the chances open to young people to earn part-time while studying, even the ability of the

19

economy to provide people from other countries with the opportunity to gain worthwhile work-experience here, these too are, arguably, constituent elements of a higher 'standard of living'. They are, certainly, no mean achievements for a country where the despondency and depression of the late 1980s and early 1990s provided fertile soil for fatalism and defeatism to take root. 'Work is dying', 'we have too many young people', 'we have too much technology', 'the Single European Market will draw companies and jobs off the island', were not as seductive perspectives on social developments at the end of decade as at the beginning. On the contrary, a decent job for everybody who wanted one, measures to attract skilled Irish people back from overseas, co-operation within companies in seizing the opportunities presented by new technologies and the Single European Market, these were widely accepted as valid objectives as the 1990s ended.

35. A proper appreciation of the scale, depth and human quality of Ireland's economic transformation in the 1990s, therefore, can help Irish society face the challenges of the beginning of the twenty-first century with greater solidarity and compassion. It should deepen a sense of wonder and gratitude that so many factors worked to pull the Irish economy in the one direction and to distance the 1990s from the 1980s by much more than the count of intervening years can suggest. It underlines how solidly based is the change in Ireland's fortunes, such that it is entirely appropriate that people should now be asked to consider and welcome wholly new policies affecting many areas of their lives. It demonstrates just how much can be achieved when social partnership is worked hard for and effectively implemented. It should help the country move into the new century without euphoria but quietly confident as a people, and with greater compassion towards those whose lives continue to be mired in hardship, both at home and overseas.

PART THREE

Looking Around

3.0   *The need for frank appraisal*

36.   The need for frank dialogue and honest appraisal is nowhere greater than in trying to answer the vexed question: who is benefiting from the surge in Ireland's economy, and who is not? While the bustle on the streets of practically every city and town and the impressive counts of builders' cranes on many skylines point to widespread prosperity, it is a prosperity that is far from universal. The level and nature of the demand being experienced at social services centres, hostels for the homeless, health board clinics, the conferences of the Society of St Vincent de Paul, and the premises and help-lines of many other voluntary organisations, underscore a point consistently made by studies of poverty in Ireland,[13] namely that social disadvantage and poverty are deeply entrenched. If Irish society does not bring resources, creativity and political determination to bear on their resolution *each decade,* it will begin to lose the battle. Along with economic and social transformations, poverty too changes its face, and measures to combat it must adapt accordingly.

37.   For Ireland to think that its new wealth as a nation justifies it placing combating poverty further down the list of priorities would be to miss key lessons of international experience. More actual failure and squalor can accompany rapid economic growth, produced by the inability of people to cope with the greater demands of economic life, and by the inward migration of those attracted to wealth. More fundamentally, markets, on their own, invariably widen inequalities. Put simply, they give the biggest rewards to those who already have the most and push out those who have the least by giving no rewards at all.[14] The greater the role that society gives markets, the greater the attention that is needed to ensure that all people are educated and equipped to participate in them on an equal basis, and that their public regulation is thoroughly effective. Poverty,

therefore, will increase unless there is a constant attention to reducing it.

38. Not all issues of current social neglect can be dealt with in this Letter, and the treatment of those that are is by no means exhaustive. Selected issues are addressed, however, to demonstrate the extent of the moral challenges with which rapid economic growth is confronting Irish society, and the urgency of the need for all its members to commit themselves anew to the common good.

3.1 Priority to the common good

39. The concept of the common good has a pivotal place in Catholic Social Teaching. It has been authoritatively described as 'the sum total of all those conditions of social life which enable individuals, families and organisations to achieve complete and effective fulfilment' (*Gaudium et Spes,* 74).[15] These 'conditions of social life' refer to people's ability to have a home, found a family, earn a livelihood, live in good health and reasonable security, and play a respected part in the life of their community. Serving the common good means seeking the social conditions that provide a truly adequate framework to life, one that enables people and their families find fulfilment and experience living in an orderly, prosperous and healthy society. In short, it protects what many people would describe as a society that is good to, and fair for, everyone.

40. The set of social conditions constituting the common good is itself shaped by the circumstances of the society in which people are living. It is inherently linked to human rights. The consciousness and acceptance of universal human rights has become steadily more widespread during the second half of the twentieth century, perhaps one of the most heartening developments of all during it. From the dignity of the human person and the one fundamental right to life are derived the rights of every person to those conditions that make a dignified human existence possible: 'Every person has the right to live…and to the means necessary for maintaining a decent

standard of living' (*Pacem in Terris,* 11).[16] This newer tradition does not dispense with the need for the concept of the common good. On the one hand, a deeper understanding and acceptance of human rights serves to clarify the social conditions that make up the common good and dispose people better to honour its demands. The common good retains, however, a characteristic emphasis on the mutual relatedness of the concepts of person and community – the 'perfection' of one cannot take place without that of the other. It is a reminder that what each individual person has a right to expect from society is also something the individual is obliged to support society in ensuring for all its members equally. It promotes a lively awareness that others' rights are the source of one's own obligations.

41. The common good is not automatically served by market forces. Without at all denying the positive role of markets, including the social advances they make possible, it is important that more people in Ireland expect and support the public authorities to intervene resolutely wherever it is necessary to protect the common good. The extent to which the country's rapid economic growth is due to opening the economy to more intense competition in wider markets underlines the need for constant vigilance. There is disconcerting evidence from other countries of how rapid growth through deeper integration into today's global economy creates winners and losers inside the same national society.[17] New energy and inventiveness are needed to find measures that deliver what the common good demands where markets plainly do not. An observation by the Catholic Bishops of England and Wales prompted by the experience in Britain is valid for Ireland too: 'The first duty of the citizen towards the common good is to ensure that nobody is marginalised (by market forces) and to bring back into a place in the community those who have been marginalised in the past'.[18] Ireland's new circumstances make it more imperative than ever that each citizen speak and act with a much greater acknowledgement of, and sense of co-responsibility for, the common good.

42. Promoting the common good is a civic obligation which Christians in particular should excel in meeting because they also make an option for the poor and a commitment to social justice. These should dispose them to be exceptionally attentive to the neglect of human need and the denial of human rights. After all, Christian faith teaches us that being human is to be part of each other; in the words of Pope John Paul II, 'we are *all* really responsible *for all*' (*Sollicitudo Rei Socialis*, 38).[19] Promoting the common good in today's context of rapidly changing social conditions, new opportunities, new threats and a deepening understanding of what makes for full human living, requires the exercise of greater solidarity than ever by Irish men and women. Solidarity has been defined precisely as '*a firm and persevering determination* to commit oneself to the common good' (*Sollicitudo Rei Socialis*, 38).

3.2 Housing and homelessness

43. Perhaps the most evident example of a conflict between market forces and the common good being exposed by the economic boom is in the housing 'market'. Nothing has so disturbed some people, and brought them to question what economic growth is really for, as the prospect that they or their children might never be able to occupy, let alone own, their own home. Several factors, some of them foreseeable, have driven the demand for housing steadily upwards. The principal ones are the growing proportion of the population in the age-bracket where setting up a household is most likely (ages 25-44), and the shift towards more one-person and two-person households. Natural growth in the population and in-migration are additional sources of demand, but it remains the fact that social and cultural changes more than having 'extra' people in the country produced the crisis of the late 1990s. In the greater Dublin area, for example, the population level is forecast to rise by 17 per cent between 2000 and 2011, but the number of its households by 50 per cent.[20] More of the Irish population overall are living in small households, partly because they can afford it and want to, and partly because marital and family relationships are less stable.

44. This rising demand far outstripped the growth in the supply of housing during the 1990s for reasons that became well known. While the construction industry expanded rapidly, the supply of serviced building land and the efficiency of the planning process constituted critical bottlenecks; land zoned for residential purposes, with water and sewerage services, good road access and public transport points, could not be speedily provided. The country came to regret the extent to which the supply of public housing was one of the casualties of fiscal cutbacks in the 1980s. Expert reports further identified how the psychology of price expectations, speculative investment switching into residential property, and falling interest rates, threw fuel on the price rises that were, to some extent, largely inevitable.[21] The scale of the price rises, however, staggered everyone. From being among the cheapest in Europe in 1989, Irish houses soared to be among the most expensive by 1999; a typical urban home that had cost 11.3 times average annual disposable income in 1989 was costing 18.2 times the average by 1999.[22]

45. The unevenness of the process of economic growth, and the arbitrary distribution of some of its benefits, are vividly demonstrated in how people have been affected by this surge in house prices. To a large number of home owners it has brought a windfall wealth effect, and a fortunate few have been able to capitalise on the soaring values of their homes. A widening range of personal investors have bought apartments and houses, some influenced primarily by the prospect of a short-term capital gain, and this has increased the difficulty of first-time buyers in getting a first foothold.[23] There is even the scandal of land banks, suitable for housing, sitting unused because their owners prefer to watch their capital accumulate rather than release them for development.[24] At the other extreme, there is clear evidence that people on low to average incomes have been squeezed out of the mortgage market (despite lower interest rates) as house prices soared.[25] As people on low to average incomes have had to abandon their hopes – for the moment at least – of buying their own home and enter the private rented sector, those below them have fared even worse. Local authority

housing lists have lengthened, homelessness has increased, help towards rent and mortgage supplements have driven up health boards' welfare expenditure, and involuntary emigration is again being fuelled.[26]

46. The housing crisis is enormously compounding the difficulties of statutory authorities and voluntary organisations in combating homelessness. Satisfactory accommodation is increasingly difficult and costly for them to provide as land and rental values have escalated. Meanwhile, family instability, the drugs problem and the number of people leaving institutional care have each acted to swell the pool of homeless people. Adult homelessness is associated in many people's minds with crippling personal problems. Drug users, alcoholics, people with psychiatric illness or who suffered trauma in their childhood run particularly high risks of falling through the nets of family ties and ordinary social services, but the homeless population is, in fact, extremely diverse. It includes a high proportion of women with children doubled up in other people's homes as well as unemployed single men making use of hostels; it includes people with prison records as well as the victims of unique constellations of misfortune in their family and business lives. In recent years, a growing number of young people, including girls and children, are leaving their homes, sometimes to the bewilderment of caring parents and sometimes fleeing extreme tensions in the home.[27] There are few areas where the demands of the common good are more transparent than here. Every support should be forthcoming to the statutory authorities and voluntary organisations working in this area to enable them develop, in as co-ordinated and effective a manner as possible, the full range of services required by the homeless population.

47. It is not appropriate that this Letter attempt to make a technical contribution to the energetic search under-way to find means of increasing housing supply and removing those elements of demand that serve no social purpose. It is in keeping with its purpose, however, to observe how deep are the changes in attitudes needed throughout society if new housing policies that serve the common good are to be formulated and

find support. For example, there probably is public support for stronger powers of compulsory acquisition, with whatever constitutional changes may be required. While several policy changes being advocated are wholly new and, in the eyes of some, 'against the grain', they are to be commended as capable of protecting social inclusion and fairness in the new national circumstances. For example, it is argued that the private rented sector should be encouraged to grow further in scale and quality, and that the need is transparent and urgent to ensure everyone's tenure is protected more fairly by law.[28] Hopes are expressed that the public housing sector – which has been steadily reduced over the years and confined to an increasingly socially disadvantaged group – may, like the private rented sector, also begin to grow in breadth and depth.[29] Calls are being made for greater public incentives to be provided to voluntary organisations to take a higher profile in providing social housing.[30] Local authorities are paying much greater attention to the desirability of achieving a wider social mix in housing patterns, and to countering the concentration of people with the lowest incomes in estates which then become stigmatised. The Government is proposing that up to 20 per cent of all lands (over a half-acre) zoned for housing should be available to local authorities for social or affordable housing.[31] There is active interest in raising the density of housing on sites that enjoy particularly good public transport links and access to amenities, and in countering public fears that higher density means high rise and poor quality.[32]

48.   These types of policy innovation are highlighted in this Letter because, to some extent, a public education deficit exists that could slow down change and compound the difficulties of the 'housing poor'. The desire of the vast majority of Irish people to own their own home is often remarked on, and is regarded as a powerful element in Ireland's political culture. However, private rented accommodation and social housing can no longer be considered forms of tenure that bring fewer social benefits than home ownership; public support to people needing a home, therefore, must become 'tenure neutral'. The objective that serves the common good here is, surely, the

achievement of 'mixed housing for mixed communities', that is, the creation of neighbourhoods where home-owners and people renting, variously, from the local authority, private landlords and housing associations are together, without anyone even needing to know who is who.[33] These reflections are not in any way intended to 'knock' the desirability of home ownership, but to lessen the chances that the political arithmetic generated by the current massive dominance of home ownership will be exploited to block changes that are in the interests of the common good.

3.3   Stewardship of the environment

49.   It is difficult to find an example of an economic activity that does not require the expenditure of energy, the occupation of space, the consumption of materials, movement by people and the generation of waste. This environmental impact may be minimal, as when a teleworker writes a report at home to be sent by electronic mail, or major, as where a large manufacturing plant needs large inputs of energy, water and the constant arrival and departure of heavy vehicles.

50.   Ireland's physical and natural environments – its roads and bridges, inland waterways and coastal waters, flora and fauna – are registering the multiple impacts of the huge increase in the volume of economic activity being undertaken on the island. The country is being forced to act quickly to ensure that irreparable damage is not done to the environment, and that raising the standard of living of the current generation is not at the expense of the quality of air and water, landscapes and general experience of nature, available to future generations.

51.   There is enormous responsibility on the public authorities to accelerate and co-ordinate the development of better public transport (especially urban), the attainment of EU standards in the treatment of waste water and provisions for solid waste, and the honouring of other international commitments entered into to protect the world's environment.[34] It is an inescapable part of the global context to Ireland's economic

boom that the level and nature of the economic activity being engaged in by the wealthy minority of the world's population is responsible for posing serious strains on the carrying capacity of the earth's eco-systems. The planet, in some instances, is already crying 'halt!' before a large part of the human family has even escaped poverty.

52. These national and global pressures make it imperative that each person become more conscious of the fragility of the physical and natural environments and show a greater sense of co-responsibility for protecting them. They are bequeathed from past generations and, in turn, should be handed on to coming generations, ennobled and not disfigured. Christians, in addition, are reminded that humanity must not think it can make 'arbitrary use of the earth, subjecting it without restraint to (human) will, as though it did not have its own requisites and a prior God-given purpose...' (*Centesimus Annus*, 37). Ireland's physical planning, its patterns of housing, the financing of water supplies, the recycling of waste, and so much else, have to be greatly developed if they are to catch up with best practice in other small countries that have successfully combined strong economic performance with protection and enhancement of their environments. That will require enlightened support from citizens, as voters, taxpayers, and members of resident associations, for the necessary public policies. In addition, there are many voluntary decisions individuals can make as householders and consumers (in the area of transport, for example) which would be a significant contribution on their part to making further economic growth less demanding on the environment.[35]

3.4 *Income adequacy and poverty*

53. The economic boom, by making huge inroads into unemployment, has helped to make inroads into poverty too. In the past, the virulence of the unemployment problem appeared to swamp all efforts to reduce the scale of poverty in Ireland; in 1987, 16 per cent of the Irish population were considered to be 'consistently poor', and studies showed

unemployment to be the chief culprit.[36] When the situation was reviewed in 1994, the percentage in **consistent poverty** had scarcely changed – it stood at 15 per cent – despite seven intervening years of good economic growth. The main reason was that unemployment had remained persistently high.[37]

54. It has been heartening that new data that became available in 1999 estimated the percentage of Irish households in consistent poverty to have fallen to 10 per cent by 1997. National poverty, by this measure, was cut by one third in less than four years.[38] This is good news and, undoubtedly, greater access to employment played the key role in achieving it; economic growth rates approximately doubled after 1994 but employment grew nearly four times faster than between 1987 and 1993.[39] Rising unemployment had fuelled poverty in the 1980s; rising employment cut it in the 1990s. We recall the convictions of many who spoke to us during the preparation of *Work is the Key* (1992) that creating jobs and ensuring that unemployed people could access them were then the main priorities in fighting poverty.

55. Is the rising tide lifting even those boats that appeared to be holed by poverty? The metaphor hides more than it reveals when applied to the reduction in the number of people who had been described as consistently poor in 1994. Consistent poverty equips no one to find and hold a job, even in an employment expansion. What success there has been, therefore, can be considered a tribute to the tireless efforts and constant consultation and co-operation practised by poor people themselves, and the voluntary and community groups, statutory agencies and professionals working with them. Poverty is not solved without greater resources being devoted to it, but neither is it solved by money alone. A family is only rescued from a history of low income and debt, an early school leaver only returns to quality education or training, a long-term unemployed person only gets and holds a good job, when their best efforts are met at each turn by sympathetic and capable individuals able to ensure that their efforts translate into concrete achievement.

56. The evidence cited of a major reduction in 'consistent poverty' does not mean there is only good news. It also estimates that one in ten Irish households were still experiencing serious deprivation, at a time when the national economy was booming around them. As significantly, the same data also point to continuing – even accelerating – growth in serious **income inequalities** within Irish society. For example, the percentage of the population living on incomes below one-half of society's average disposable income was 21 per cent in 1994 but 22 per cent in 1997. Ireland's rapid economic growth is leaving some people behind, and catching others up, more quickly than ever. It has never been such a bad time to have no educational qualifications or be seeking a first home, and never such a good time to be graduating from a university or to own several properties. The 'relative' income poverty that can worsen as a result should not be lightly dismissed, nor assumed to be largely a temporary phenomenon. Living on an income far below what most others enjoy can bite painfully; a person may feel, and be perceived by others to be, a failure.

57. Furthermore, there are other measures of poverty that look not just to absolute or relative income but to factors apart altogether from money that influence how well, if at all, a person can play a role in society. For example, not being able to read or write satisfactorily, being jobless for years on end, being unable to have a satisfactory place to live, having a disability for which workplaces and public places are not adjusted, also denote a real impoverishment in today's Ireland. Combinations of some of these measures of social exclusion suggest that over *one-fifth* of the Irish population are being kept from the mainstream of Irish life.[40]

58. Further sustained reductions in the proportion of the Irish population living in poverty are, without doubt, going to be more difficult to achieve. There is no room for complacency, but the road travelled can give strength for the road ahead. An important lesson from studies of poverty in Ireland is that its causes are multiple and intertwined: the grind of living on a low income over a long stretch of time runs down assets,

restricts socialising and participation in various networks, replaces savings with debts, erodes workplace skills, undermines self-confidence, can alienate even family and friends, and indirectly leads to poor health. Such multiple deprivation is deep-rooted; it will not be – and has not been – banished by even a decade of rapid growth.

59. Societies with which Ireland has particularly close contacts, the US and the UK, feature prominently in international league tables for the extent of the earnings and income inequalities that they tolerate. Sadly, Ireland is typically close to them in these tables.[41] At the same time, Ireland is also like smaller Continental European countries in other respects. The International Labour Organisation cited Ireland, along with Austria, Denmark and the Netherlands, as an example of a country where significant employment growth had been achieved **using** the traditions of the European welfare state model: 'They all have a well-established net of social protection, and practise a social dialogue and social partnership, with a rather assertive role for governments. Their labour market institutions and welfare arrangements have been strengthened through an adaptation to new needs'.[42] In fact, Ireland could be said to be attempting to forge its own social model, one that combines the labour market flexibility of the Anglo-Saxon economies with the social cohesiveness and greater egalitarianism of the Continental EU States. Firmly inside the EU as it is, Ireland can offer and receive in the ongoing quest to reshape EU social policy. The rapid employment expansion of recent years, as noted, has been beneficial for social cohesion, and other European countries understandably now study Ireland in this regard. However, in Ireland, the State guarantees a relatively low floor to incomes alongside a relatively narrow tax base, and tolerates wide differences in the standards of basic health care and education by comparison to the standards of many other small EU member States. These are areas in which they constitute an example to this country.

60. In the midst of the economic boom, the nation's first National

Anti-Poverty Strategy was produced (1997).[43] The timing was indebted to the United Nations Social Summit in Copenhagen in 1995, which had strengthened the voice of those fighting poverty and brought the Irish Government to make commitments in this regard to the international community. Under this Strategy, Government departments and public bodies have assumed the responsibility of 'poverty proofing' their policies and of practising a structured accountability, in particular to those of Ireland's citizens living on the lowest incomes; the Strategy is to be reviewed during the year 2000.[44] It is a welcome development. It would be a lost opportunity if other pressures and demands generated by rapid economic growth should distract Government or the public sector from the importance of the review. The energy and effectiveness with which the Strategy is pursued have clear potential for further reducing poverty and, thus, enhancing the quality of life for everyone.

3.5 Long-term unemployment

61. Even a rapidly growing economy cannot be expected wholly to eliminate unemployment. The very changes that make growth possible mean that a significant number of people will be constantly in the process of retraining, relocating or searching for the job that maximises the use of their skills. But, apart from this 'frictional unemployment', Ireland ended the 1990s with a substantial number of people still in a situation of long-term unemployment, minimally some 2 to 3 per cent of the total labour force and possibly much more.[45] By international standards, this is high and an extremely formidable challenge. It is a particularly acute moral challenge because much of this long-term unemployment is the fruit of a double legacy, namely an under-investment in education in the past and the ravages of an overall unemployment rate that was above 10 per cent almost uninterruptedly for twenty-five years.

62. Ireland began to invest substantially in secondary education much later than other Northern European countries, with the result that a large proportion of its older workers today have no

secondary qualifications whatsoever. While there is much emphasis on, and pride in, the levels of attainment of the young Irish leaving the educational system and joining the workforce, the gap between the skills profile of this inflow and what characterises the overall workforce is still immense.[46] In fact, Ireland stands out among countries in Northern Europe for having the highest proportion of its labour force *without* second-level qualifications. It was bottom of a list of ten industrial countries in 1995 for the percentage of its working-age population who were functionally illiterate, in the sense of 'lacking an ability to read and write adequate for the most basic demands of modern society, such as reading instructions on a medicine bottle or reading stories to children'.[47]

63. While the high unemployment of the 1980s has been massively reduced, its effects are still very present in Irish society – in the lives of individuals and families who slowly and painfully learned to cope by adapting their expectations and shaping their lives around joblessness. It needs to be remembered how the rate of long-term unemployment in Ireland was higher for years than the total unemployment rates of other countries, which yet considered themselves to have an unemployment 'problem'. The exceptional duration of unemployment for some people is captured in the observation that a small number of them accounted for a huge proportion of 'unemployed time'; between 1980 and 1987, 50 per cent of unemployment measured in person-days was lived by 4 per cent of the population.[48] The severity of this crisis made deep inroads into people's self-esteem, expectations, lifestyles, skills, and into local communities.[49]

64. This double legacy of poor literacy and numeracy skills characterising the older population and of an adjustment to joblessness that went on over many years, continues to require immense consultation, imagination and energy to overcome. Some of the evidence as to how long-term unemployed people fared during the 1990s is disappointing.[50] For example, they benefited little from training initiatives and were the least likely to be found on quality training programmes and the

most likely to be found on programmes that had only weak links with the mainstream labour market. A relatively large proportion left unemployment only in the sense that they transferred to other welfare schemes or participated on the Community Employment programme. However, new developments give ground for hope.[51] More quality training is being routed towards them as of 1998. More of them are experiencing that taking a job brings a genuine improvement in their financial circumstances. Community organisations, local partnerships and the statutory agencies are co-operating more intensely through the Local Employment Service to reach them and accompany them on their sometimes long route back to gainful employment. It would be unacceptable if anything were to downplay the particular moral claim this disadvantaged group has on Ireland's new resources.

65. These reflections may temper the indignation of those who point to considerable long-term unemployment and job vacancies existing side by side. It is perplexing that a large number of people remain unemployed at a time when labour shortages have developed for low-skilled work also, and employers are actively recruiting overseas. Some commentators charge that those remaining long-term unemployed contain a large number of people who do not want a job. Others express concern that employers may be turning to overseas recruitment too readily, and that people who are long-term unemployed are not being fairly considered as potential workers whom quality training and a measure of accompaniment would bring back into the mainstream economy. They charge that there are employers running modern services outlets who simply do not want many among the unemployed on grounds of age, background and lack of the desired social skills.

66. It is right that unemployed people today be expected to seek and accept fair and reasonable offers of employment. However, it needs to be remembered how the lowest skilled among them were led to believe, for many years, that they simply were not needed, that the jobs on offer to them are often insecure or short-term, and that the step to training can be as difficult for

them as the step into a job. The need is for patience, tolerance, and endless inventiveness and imagination to prove to individuals themselves that, indeed, no one is 'unemployable'. The fall in unemployment is an opportunity to concentrate on the quality rather than the scale of labour market programmes, and to guarantee meaningful progression to better outcomes for long-term unemployed people who participate in them. Employers in particular should appreciate how great is the social good they serve when they view low-skilled, unemployed people who are over 40 as an under-used resource, and privilege them in their recruitment and company training.[52] There has been a good response to programmes that rely on genuinely widening the options open to long-term unemployed people (the Back to Work Allowance, Area Based Enterprise Allowance, Back to Education Allowance, etc.), rather than on restricting their options. This justifies – we believe – the perspective adopted by *Work is the Key:* healthy people with a healthy relationship to their society tend spontaneously to want and seek work. People who are long-term unemployed, community-based organisations and statutory bodies can truly be described as working for the one objective: the unfolding of human work to the benefit of persons and society.[53]

3.6   *Early school leavers*

67.   While Ireland's booming economy, oriented towards services, has not notably recruited the older among the long-term unemployed, the opposite is the case for young people whose level of educational attainment is still low-level relative to their age cohort. As the 1990s drew to a close, they were getting jobs with greater ease, and at higher wages, than their counterparts in the 1980s ever experienced.[54] The demand in the economy today for young people with relatively low levels of skill is now acknowledged in several quarters as a type of perverse incentive, one that is leading to under-involvement in education and sowing the seeds of the long-term unemployment of the future.[55] It is not just early school-leavers who are having their incentive or interest in returning to education undermined in this way. The performance **at school**

of some students is being seriously affected by the hours they are putting in on part-time jobs. Sometimes the pressure to earn arises from genuine financial needs in the youngsters' households, sometimes it is driven by the rising expectations of the young people themselves and the ease with which a wage packet can be spent.

68. This new financial reason making it attractive to leave school is superimposed on the more persistent nature of other early school-leaving. Ever since the introduction of free second-level schooling, the secondary education system has had difficulty in adjusting to the wider range of pupil abilities that this entailed. The lowest achieving 25 per cent of students have continued to be in particular danger of experiencing failure rather than success, and of becoming more conscious of a level of academic ability they lack rather than coming to appreciate their other strengths. Not surprisingly, a wage packet – and even the fact that a workplace is giving them a positive experience of working with others – is a particularly strong attraction to them.

69. To some extent, a society that places enormous emphasis on independence, earning and the benefits of consumption is poorly placed to preach restraint to young people for whom the opportunities to earn and spend appear wide open. Several national measures are already being considered to address this new problem: raising the school-leaving age, requiring employers to provide education or training for workers under 18, and ensuring that low-income families do not have a lower standard of living simply because a young person is remaining in school. However, it is just as important that families and schools redouble their efforts to convey to young people that life is about so much more than consumption and a 'standard of living'. This is a time for increased dialogue between parents, teachers, educational authorities and employers to improve the balance between education as an investment in future earnings potential and education as the foundation for a full, human life.

70. The sense that the good times are by-passing sections of the population is closely connected to the stubborn persistence of 'poverty black spots' in Ireland's cities.[56] These are inner-city areas and public housing estates on the edges of cities and towns that continue to contain high concentrations of vulnerable households: lone parents, large families being reared on low incomes, older low-skilled workers with health problems, and elderly people on social welfare pensions. Residents who are in the workforce tend to have poor educational qualifications, to have held mainly low-skilled employments, to run high risks of unemployment, and to receive only offers of low-paid, intermittent employment. A surprisingly large percentage of their overall populations, thus, have little cause to travel outside their area in the course of the day and the immediate physical environment – frequently visually depressing with limited amenities and poor shopping facilities – accordingly impacts on them strongly. Schools located in these areas can struggle with exceptionally high rates of early school leaving, and health board clinics with heavy demand. The majority of their households are without cars, yet car-use frequently dominates the local landscape (tiered car parks and through-traffic in inner cities, the proximity of busy roads in peripheral estates). The low housing density on some of the larger estates, and their sprawling road layout with frequent culs-de-sac, make efficient bus services difficult to provide. There is either an absence of large employers locally (the case of some peripheral estates), or a wealth of employment that local residents are singularly ill-equipped to take (inner-city communities beside business districts).[57]

71. These urban black spots are largely the indirect result of wider national policies. The zoning of industry away from city centres reduced much of the employment on which inner city populations had traditionally depended. The construction of large public housing estates on city perimeters resulted in many young households without the support of extended family networks and in populations bereft, for years at least, of

an adequate range of amenities and services. The shrinking of the local authority housing stock resulted in it being increasingly reserved for households with exceptional social needs. About eight out of ten local authority tenants were welfare-dependent by the mid-1990s; in cities, they were thirty times more likely to be poor than owner-occupiers in the private sector. (In Dublin, for example, there was an almost one-in-two chance of a local authority tenant being poor in 1994).[58] This has helped give public housing areas a reputation for social problems and social disorganisation. The financial incentives to home ownership, and the natural desire to improve their children's educational prospects, further bled these areas of their residents with the better incomes and more secure jobs. As the 1990s ended, these disadvantaged areas still appeared as largely de-linked from the more thriving and prosperous cities and towns around them.

72. It is in these urban black spots that using and supplying drugs appear to have their strongest attractions. The problem grew steadily after 1990 and the proportion treated for heroin abuse, a drug particularly associated with crime and deaths, had doubled by 1996. By the mid-1990s, a quarter of all reported drug misuse in the State was taking place in Dublin's inner city.[59] An extensive study of the extreme spatial concentration of social disadvantage in Dublin in the late 1970s had warned: 'if cities do not deal constructively with poverty, poverty will deal destructively with cities'.[60] Many community workers have observed that the subsequent arrival of drugs effectively turned some people's anger at their unemployment and social marginalisation in on themselves, their families and neighbourhoods.

73. The profile of drug-users is depressingly clear: they tend to be unemployed young men, many of whom left school early.[61] The overwhelming majority of them began abusing drugs while in their teens, a good number under the age of 15; it appears that the young age of Ireland's drug-using population is notable by European standards. Even where parents, teachers, community workers and statutory officials are

working closely together to halt misuse, supply appears capable of producing its own demand. Local Drugs Task Forces[62] are engaged in a united and vigorous local response, but the evil they tackle has roots far beyond their areas. A near hysteria towards drug-users in some sections of the community does much to make their work more difficult, and misses the crucial point that – however unpredictable and dangerous is the behaviour of an individual under the influence of drugs, however battered and miserable his or her appearance – the addict is someone's son or daughter.[63] No one, drug misusers, their parents or their children, should have to walk alone or suffer in the silence of fear or shame. The large numbers waiting for entry to a detoxification programme represent so many people attempting the huge step away from drug use; treatment that restores self-respect and hope for the future through therapy, education and retraining ought to be a real option open to all of them.[64] A society that does not speedily lend them the necessary helping hand in every way possible is showing a blinkered perception of its own long-term good.

74. Urban areas with concentrations of social need are highly visible. While this can help the mobilisation and targeting of help, it also generates a damaging stigma. When the Irish economy was floundering, the conditions of life in the same disadvantaged urban areas were routinely 'discovered' by the national and international media, and used as introductions to commentaries on unemployment, drugs, crime, the alienation of youth, or whatever. In many ways, the recognition was slow in coming that the greatest assets, in fighting the disproportionate incidences in these areas of what are national problems, are precisely the commitment, expertise and values of the people living in them. It is still insufficiently appreciated outside of them that they tend, in fact, to be characterised by a high degree of neighbourliness and sense of community.[65] There has consistently been a community response within these areas to the heavy incidences of social disadvantage that they carry and, during the 1990s, these responses were supported in an unprecedented way by national and EU programmes.[66] It is a tribute to the residents in these areas that

they come together, to the extent that they do, to show solidarity with each other, insist on their statutory rights, create new services and try to reverse social discrimination against them. The degree to which they activated what are called special labour market programmes is an important part of the story of how Ireland overcame high unemployment.

75. The economic boom has brought increased difficulties for Ireland's urban black spots. Standards in the wider society have, in many respects, pulled further ahead, emphasising their relative deprivation. The expectations of the people in these areas are rising, as much as anywhere else, and financial indebtedness is becoming more serious. The national crises in housing and public transport are impacting on them strongly. The labour market programmes, on which many of their community organisations have depended for mounting their services, are being changed and scaled down. Advertised job vacancies in the city compound the frustration of lone parents unable to find satisfactory childcare and of older low-skilled men plainly unsuited to many of the new jobs.

76. But there is hope also. Some individuals in these urban black spots are benefiting from the national upsurge in employment, principally young people with at least a Junior Certificate and women returning to work who are able to arrange childcare. Many local authorities have reappraised their approach to housing management and regard working with and through local residents as vital to ensuring the successful regeneration of an estate. The Integrated Services Project is designed to increase the effectiveness of statutory bodies and to ensure that the standards of public services available locally are equal to those available in more fortunate parts of cities. Some large urban renewal projects reflect a holistic approach and concern to include local populations in their planning and implementation; they constitute a major advance on projects exclusively concerned with property values and rental incomes.[67]

77. Finally, there is a widening appreciation that the persistence of areas of multiple deprivation may act as a brake on a city's

continuing prosperity, as the regional economy shifts increasingly to knowledge- and services-based industries. The overall quality of life offered by a city has become important to its economic success. Expensive housing, long commuting times, a scarcity of childcare facilities, long waiting lists for schools, high crime levels, a dearth of green spaces and pleasant parks, now mean that skilled workers may decline job opportunities and choose to live elsewhere. This influences the companies who seek to recruit them and, thus, the flow of inward investment.[68] Socially disadvantaged populations in Irish cities have some solid grounds for hoping that the private sector will now support larger and more imaginative interventions that complement their own community efforts and, thus, help bring to an end constant new versions of 'tales of two cities'.

3.8   Rural disadvantage

78.   While urban Ireland has struggled to cope with more people and cars, factors associated with the economic boom, and others independent of it, have compounded the difficulties of isolated rural areas in retaining their populations and the minimum range of social services necessary for community living. Urban investors have helped to push local property prices far beyond the range of local house-seekers and land prices out of the reach of small and medium-sized farmers seeking to consolidate their holdings. While this has brought a once-off benefit to those in a position to sell, it has enormously compounded the already disadvantaged position of the landless, and further endangered the ability of local communities to retain their own new generations. In addition, in some areas, a growing incidence of holiday homes, by being empty for much of the year, further threatens the viability of the local community.[69] Independently of the boom, rural areas also suffered after 1994 from a collapse in agricultural incomes, constraints on the fishing industry and continuing emigration.[70] A significant part of the rural population can truly feel that descriptions of Ireland's economic transformation in the 1990s are of 'somewhere over there'.[71]

79. Many people are aware that the proportion of the Irish population living in the capital city and its hinterland is unusually high by European standards. Fewer may appreciate that the proportion still living in rural areas – defined as open countryside and villages and towns of less than 3000 persons – is also unusually high, and the population density there exceptionally sparse, by international standards. Rural disadvantage, therefore, deserves emphasis simply because of the scale of human need in the Irish countryside, and not because the rural population is claiming any symbolic or residual historic claim over urban Ireland.

80. Dublin city and county contained some 30 per cent of the country's poorest households in 1994, but rural areas contained 36 per cent of them. In addition, the highest **risk** of poverty at that time was faced by the part of the rural population living in the smallest villages and towns.[72] A second example of the social need 'hidden' in the Irish countryside is educational disadvantage. While it is the focus of particular and merited attention in urban areas, data from the early 1990s established that – in numerical terms at least – educational disadvantage is predominantly a rural phenomenon, with three out of five disadvantaged pupils living in small towns or the open countryside where the problem is less visible and proving even harder to tackle.[73] A final example is that of the elderly living alone. Their difficulties are enormously compounded when circumstances make visiting others, or being visited by them, more difficult. This is just what the absence of public transport, ongoing depopulation and the centralisation of services in the larger towns have done for many of the elderly living alone in rural Ireland. In addition, the quality of their housing tends to be poorer than that of the elderly who live alone in urban areas; one study found that more than a quarter had no bath/shower in their home and a fifth no indoor toilet (the corresponding figures for the urban elderly living alone were 7 and 2 per cent respectively).[74]

81. Being poor in a rural area avoids some of the indignities of urban blight but, on the other hand, can entail a hugely

damaging isolation. It is, frequently, to feel, and be, utterly alone without the means (especially transport) or the confidence to take part in what is happening under the banner of 'community'. It can also mean it is practically impossible to access those services that help a person begin the long, hard climb out of social disadvantage (adult literacy programmes, personal development courses, participation in group activities, skills training, etc.). Tribute is due to the volunteers working in rural development organisations of every sort for the long hours and extraordinary mileage put in by them in an effort to include the most marginalised individuals in the developments of their areas.[75]

82. Like much else in contemporary Ireland, there is a strong sense that the quality of rural life is being shaped now for generations to come. It is good that the issue is clearly focused as a much broader one than the future of Irish agriculture; already, two out of three rural dwellers are not directly dependent on farming.[76] However, the numbers and the economic and social functions of farmers remain hugely important to ensuring vibrant and balanced rural communities. Successive studies have confirmed a picture of wide differences between Irish farms. For example, only 31 per cent merited a clear classification as economically viable in the mid 1990s; their average family farm income was eight times greater than that of the bottom 20 per cent of Irish farms. The latter were firmly classified as non-viable because of their small size, lack of additional earning sources, age of the farmer (over 55) and absence of a successor. On the remaining one-half of Irish farms, much depends on the younger household members becoming able to supplement their incomes from farming with other on- and off-farm activities. There must be hope and insistence that now, unlike the operations of the commodity price-support regime and the first rounds of direct payments to farmers which began to substitute for them, further EU-inspired reforms to Irish farming (provoked by Agenda 2000 and world trade negotiations) will, at last, see the remaining smaller landholders benefiting proportionately more rather than far less, as has been the case since 1973.[77]

83. The diversity of constituencies that now take an active interest in the Irish countryside is to be welcomed. It is clear that a strong appreciation of the countryside's many features and its myriad potential is part of society's heightened environmental sensitivity. This includes: small-scale food production, organic livestock and cultivation,[78] natural habitats sheltering a diversity of species, archaeological and cultural sites, landscapes and seascapes, coastal currents and harbours, inland waterways, angling and (shell)fish-farming, forest walks and mountain ways, and so much else. The balancing of these different interests and developments is at the heart of the search for a comprehensive rural policy today. It is important that 'all people living in rural areas should be provided with the capacity to contribute and to share more equitably in the benefits of economic and social progress'.[79] Each constituency – the agricultural, the environmental, the tourist, the recreational, the mining – should be challenged to demonstrate how landless individuals, geographically isolated dwellers, the poorly educated and least skilled members of the rural workforce, the transport and housing poor, in short, the full rural population, can benefit from developments that they propose. Unspoilt and charming landscapes must cease to be the setting for lives of acute hardship and loneliness. A self-confident and socially inclusive rural society will be the best steward of a rural environment that enhances life for everyone.

3.9 *People with disabilities*

84. A significant group, for whom care was scant in time of economic recession, is the estimated 10 per cent of the Irish population who live with a disability. For many, their disability takes the form of a physical or sensory impairment, for others it is a learning difficulty, poor mental health or an emotional impairment. When account is taken of the families, friends and organisations caring for them, a major section of the population is involved. The quality of the lives of people with disabilities is vitally affected by the attitudes and organisation of the society around them; these affect, above all, the degree of independence, self-esteem and social status with which they

can live. At one extreme are people leading full lives, despite even severe impairments, because of their own determination, the care of their families, and the presence of supporting networks of voluntary and statutory personnel.[80] At the other extreme, are isolated and abandoned individuals who have fallen through every net and whose abject condition can even bring others to fear them; such are people who are mentally ill and homeless.[81] A person's disability does not have to be very severe before she or he faces increased vulnerabilty (including being taken advantage of by others), increased expenses, and mounting difficulties in finding a job.

85. The Report of the Commission on the Status of People with Disabilites concluded that public attitudes and society's failure to adapt the physical environment and its social and economic policies were the major reasons why people experienced their disabilities as disadvantages. It pointed in particular to failures to adapt buildings and transport networks, to provide appropriate information on entitlements, to tailor the delivery of health and social services, to ensure educational opportunities and access to employment.[82] For these reasons, people with disabilities were having difficulties in exercising their basic rights on an equal footing with others. The same review welcomed the shift from a medical to a social perspective on disability, as the latter exposes the imperfections and deficiencies in surrounding society. It also urged wide implementation of the United Nations' Standard Rules on the Equalisation of Opportunities for Persons with Disabilities (adopted in 1993) as a benchmark for best practice on the part of every Irish institution.

86. During the years of high unemployment and acute constraints on government spending, the special needs of people with disabilities were met, in many instances, only through the intensified efforts of families and voluntary organisations. In other instances, their needs remained unmet or even intensified, as when people were discharged from psychiatric institutions into the doomed project of living on their own without adequate supports, or where essential renovations of

public institutions were postponed. There are several ways in which public policy can be strengthened and public expenditure increased to improve directly the quality of life for all people with a disability and those who care for them; for example, improving and extending the carer's allowance, further resourcing the voluntary and statutory organisations that provide high-support accommodation and services in the community, ensuring the accessibility of public buildings and public transportation systems. However, a thorough change in public attitudes and expectations must accompany the necessary increases in expenditure. A newly prosperous Ireland should take to heart the words of Pope John Paul II: 'it would be a denial of our common humanity to admit to the life of the community, and thus admit to work, only those who are fully functional' (*Laborem Exercens,* 22).[83]

3.10 *The prison population*

87.   Poverty and acute social inequality do not determine the level of crime but they certainly create conditions that increase its occurrence. Ireland's prison population has been growing (some 2,500 people were in custody in the Irish State on an average day at the end of the decade), as has the public fear of crime. Prisoners are those people from whom society considers it must protect itself; their principal punishment is the removal of the right to free movement. As a major study of the Irish penal system pointed out in 1985, they are sent to prison **as** punishment and not **for** punishment.[84] There continue to be grounds for deep concern that the experience of being in an Irish prison still serves to distance offenders further from any chance of morally reconstructing their lives and becoming integrated into society.[85] In part, this is because Irish society was caught off-balance by the surge in crime since the late 1960s and the increasingly vicious nature of some of it, and was slow to match with resources the growing number of people it was locking away, and for longer. The country moved from being a 'policeman's paradise' to a situation where it was sending 6,000 people a year to prison by 1995, a two-fold increase on 1970. The greater vulnerability of society injected a

new harshness into the public discourse on law and order, and led to stiffer sentencing, but the necessary complementary investment in prisons and the development of non-custodial sentencing lagged far behind.

88. Mountjoy prison has been described as 'unique in Europe in terms of the throughput with which it must cope'.[86] There, it can be plainly seen how youth constitute a huge proportion of the Irish prison population (*one-third* are aged 21 or under, as against 10 per cent in the EU), and how extremely socially disadvantaged prisoners' backgrounds are. Consistently, more than one-half of Mountjoy's prisoners come from five to six deprived areas of Dublin, and from particularly large familes often broken by separation or desertion. They are overwhelmingly early school-leavers who were unemployed prior to being imprisoned. From prison, many return to prison (recidivism is remarkably high by international standards), and the proportion with a serious dependency on a hard drug doubled to 63 per cent between 1986 and 1996.[87] This bleak picture has its roots in the extraordinary difficulties disadvantaged urban communities are having in socialising young males, and has been compounded by the advent of drugs and prison overcrowding. It is sketched here, not as a plea to 'go soft' on crime, but to magnify those voices asking Irish society to be much more clear-eyed in how it seeks to protect itself.

89. Each time a court sentence is handed down, the Christian hopes for eventual reconciliation between the offender and society. This can only take place through a full acknowledgement of the damage, sometimes truly terrible, done to innocent people's lives; ways of bringing offenders to see and regret the needless pain they have inflicted must remain central to the process of reconciliation. Different forms of community service in lieu of custody deserve vigorous development, while attention to the length of prison sentences must be balanced by a concern that time in prison is used constructively and does not perpetuate an aimless existence and institutional dependence. Prisoners 'remain valued

48

members of society entitled on release to take a constructive place in society', and Christians everywhere should wholeheartedly support 'voluntary community effort to support offenders while in custody, and also to help them on release to take a full place in the community'.[88]

3.11 *Former emigrants who remained low-skilled*

90. As Ireland becomes more wealthy, it can easily forget those emigrants of earlier decades who left with few skills and never recovered from their poor start. Many are now elderly and none will be sought by Irish recruitment agencies or employers. They left reluctantly and eased conditions at home by their going; many directly helped the families and communities they left behind by sending money home. In many instances, lives of manual labour and intermittent unemployment are being finished out in social isolation and hardship. Recent research on the Irish community in Britain paints a sobering picture of disproportionate numbers of people living in difficult social situations precisely because, after emigrating, many did not successfully integrate and experienced no upward social mobility.[89] Generous support for the Irish agencies overseas or at home that work with emigrants, and measures that ease their return to Ireland where they desire that (through, for example, appropriate social housing), are the least this group might expect from Ireland's new wealth.

3.12 *The Travelling People*

91. In some respects, the situation of the Travelling People became more difficult as the economic boom got underway.[90] They have been affected by the acceleration in the development of roads and urban sites, the knock-on effects of the national shortage of housing, and the rising threshold of social skills demanded of anyone seeking employment today. In other respects, the heightened pace of economic activity is providing opportunities for Travellers too. Some are proving able to turn traditional aspects of their economic activities – skills in

recycling, preferences for self-employment and contract work, trading based on regional mobility – to their favour in the new economic times. Their preference for self-employment and to work according to their situation and circumstance have been reflected positively in writings on rural Ireland. They should be supported in every way possible in their efforts to shape an economic niche for themselves in an Ireland that has profoundly changed.

92. As national standards of every sort have improved, there has been tangible evidence of some improvements in the social conditions of the Travelling People too. This is a tribute to them and to many others. However, it should be a cause of concern to every Irish person that, going into the twenty-first century, the Travelling People still suffer from high infant mortality, low life-expectancy, extensive adult illiteracy and a high incidence of roadside living. In addition to these harsh aspects to their current lives, there is a continuing prejudice in Irish society that is a pervasive reality overshadowing the life of the Travelling Community. This prejudice can manifest itself as social exclusion of a most blatant sort, as when schools show reluctance to enrol Traveller children, hotels, bars and other leisure facilities refuse to admit Travellers, and every proposal to provide accommodation suited to them meets with vehement opposition. While Travellers are recognised by themselves and others as a distinct group, they are as Irish as anyone else.

93. The dignity of the human person and the dictates of the common good require that every member of a society have access to satisfactory accommodation, at all times. While the space and comfort afforded by the average Irish home have increased dramatically, and home ownership continued to extend, over 1,250 Traveller families still live without toilets, water, electricity or washing facilities.[91] Others live on poorly constructed and badly managed halting sites that are overcrowded and falling into disrepair. In response to this situation, and to the 1995 *Report of the Task Force on the Travelling Community,* the Government committed itself to the

implementation of a programme whereby 3,100 new units of accommodation would come on stream by the year 2000. Although the implementation of this programme has begun, progress has been painfully slow. It is important that the Task Force's recommendations are fully implemented as soon as possible. This is, surely, not an enormous challenge for the combined forces of national and local government and the voluntary sector to deliver together.[92] Securing decent accommodation for all Travellers, with the improved health and educational attainment that then become easier to ensure, remains hugely important to supporting the efforts of the many – Travellers themselves, voluntary organisations, public officials and educationalists – who are working to eradicate prejudice against them from Irish society.

94.   If more Travellers are to share in the benefits of the stronger economy, access to formal education is more essential than ever. Almost all Traveller children attend primary school – a great advance on the 1960s – but only a small percentage of them go on to second level and, of those who do, the majority leave within two years. As with any group in the Irish population, a full place in society will increasingly be undermined if education is neglected. Nothing should be spared in seeking, and delivering on, parity of educational attainment for young Travellers. This will include taking care that they find a positive attitude towards their traditions and distinctive way of life in the educational curriculum, and that their parents are helped to appreciate the significance of schooling for the futures of their children and supported in advancing their own education.

3.13 Refugees and asylum-seekers

95.   Intolerance in Irish society has found another and very different target in the growing number of asylum-seekers and refugees who have come to Ireland. These people are the living witnesses of the extent to which the twentieth century has closed with war, civil unrest, unjust government, and widespread, chronic poverty still disfiguring the human family.

As an island and a nation, Ireland experienced each of these trials in the last two hundred and fifty years. While the country firmly believes they are behind it now, peoples in Africa, Eastern Europe and the Balkans can, in no way, say the same. Refugees and asylum-seekers are uprooted from their own culture, miss deeply many people who are dear to them and struggle with the difficulties of a new language and environment. They find enforced dependence on social welfare alien to them, yet are restricted in taking up employment, with the beneficial effects that would have on themselves and others. They can appear as isolated and rootless. Some arrive suffering from post-traumatic stress. It is difficult to exaggerate their vulnerability.

96. The numbers who have come to Ireland are still small in relative terms compared to most other European States, but their arrival found Irish society unprepared. Irish people might have thought that, as a nation so long colonised, the country was a natural ally of the poorer nations of the world from its seat just inside the rich countries' club. In fact, the attitudes and behaviour of a section of the population show that, in some quarters at least, the 'Ireland of the welcomes' is a total fiction.[93] We repeat with insistence: 'Harbouring racist thoughts and attitudes is a sign against the specific message of Christ!'[94] On the positive side, however, there is heartening evidence of a national empathy forged by centuries of suffering, of the beneficial impact of the experience of the many Irish people who have lived and worked in the developing world, and of a deep assimilation of the Christian faith which has always accorded 'the stranger' a singular role in testing the quality of Christian love (Mt 25:35). Great credit is due to those people, organisations and parishes that have come forward to acknowledge the dignity of the refugees and asylum-seekers in their midst, accept their history and appreciate the cultures and peoples from which they come. Including an individual refugee or asylum-seeker today in a family, sports club, workplace, parish group, or any other type of network is a powerful statement that an equal is being embraced. It is a practical and Christian way of acknowledging

and responding to the images of famine and human displacement that television so often transmits in-between advertising and entertainment.

97. There is much still to be done to have in place an admissions system for refugees and asylum-seekers that respects Ireland's international obligations and the dictates of natural justice, and to have it functioning smoothly. It has been clearly described.[95] It should be transparent, respect due process and be fair; it should be cost-efficient and therefore speedy, adequately protect individuals whose claims are well-founded, while deterring, detecting and dealing firmly but humanely with those whose claims are not. Finally, it should provide a clearly assured status and guarantee of rights to those who are admitted. The 1996 Refugee Act needs to be fully implemented. Just legislation and fair and efficient procedures are the best protection, both of individuals fleeing from persecution for which there is 'a well-founded fear' and of Irish (and EU) society from abuse. The public authorities must take the lead in developing concerted national and local approaches that share the responsibility for receiving and supporting these vulnerable people as widely as possible across the community. In particular, a balance must be struck between enabling them to provide mutual support by remaining together, and directing them to a diversity of areas and communities where services may be under less pressure and the talents of individuals can be more easily recognised and find an outlet. Irish society must press ahead in learning how best to support refugees and asylum-seekers and integrate into its national life those who cannot return to their home countries.

PART FOUR

Looking Within

4.0 *What we mean by looking within*

98. The areas of social concern addressed in Part Three constitute evidence that the common good is not being served at all sufficiently in Ireland today; the problems reviewed are so many visible fractures in Irish society. But there are *invisible* fractures too. It is important to attend to how participating in a rapidly expanding economy can affect people's ways of thinking and seeing. The dangers of 'materialism' attach not just to the super-rich; it is a process whose inner workings can affect the lives of potentially any one of us.

99. Pope Paul VI movingly reminded the world that economic overdevelopment and moral underdevelopment are frequently found together: 'Increased possessions is not the ultimate goal of nations nor of individuals. All growth is ambivalent. It is essential if people are to develop as people, but in a way it imprisons those who consider it the supreme good, and it restricts their vision. ... Both for nations and for individuals, avarice is the most evident form of moral underdevelopment' (*Populorum Progressio,* 19).[96] It may seem premature to reflect on this phenomenon for Ireland. Though growing fast, Ireland's wealth as a nation is still considerably behind that of several countries with which it is frequently compared.[97] However, the sobering social experience of other countries, the USA in particular,[98] is a warning that it is not too early to scan Irish society for those ways of thinking and acting that, unless named and addressed, will grow and undermine people's experience and feeling that they belong to the one society and are part of each other, however market forces may rank them or discriminate between them.

4.1 *Economic progress and human happiness*

100. Countries are frequently compared on the basis of their GNP per capita. This yardstick is likely to be superseded,

over the next decade, by wider and richer measurements that incorporate indicators of a country's social achievements and environmental standards along with its economic strength.[99] Christians in particular will follow with interest these efforts to develop broader measures of the overall quality of life characterising a society. However, a different type of measure altogether – of a country's mental and spiritual health, of the overall contentment and happiness of its citizens – is so inherently difficult to compute that it is unlikely ever to be routinely published by the EU, OECD or UN. Even without good international data, the questions of most interest to people remain: Does economic growth lead to greater human happiness? Where, and for what reasons, is this more clearly the case? How does rapid economic growth appear to be affecting people's capacity to enjoy the much greater material benefits it brings them? What is it that makes some societies able to translate sustained economic growth into widespread prosperity and security, while others are fragmented by it?

101. Polls and surveys of individuals' feelings and perceptions go some way to shedding light on these questions. However, there is no easy way to gather and assess the overall picture of the state of a society that comes from marriage counsellors and child psychologists, social workers and psychiatrists, family doctors and home-school liaison workers, addiction therapists and teachers, priests, religious and other pastoral workers, the police, community welfare officers and psychoanalysts. If the changes in demand which have been made on all these professions during the 1990s in Ireland could be identified and presented as a single barometer of the 'quality of life' characterising Irish society, would it have risen or fallen? This open – perhaps unanswerable – question is on many people's minds.

4.2 *More of everything, except time?*

102. One thing that rapid economic growth undoubtedly appears to do is make **time a scarce resource**. That the opportunities

are there is a pressure of itself to seize them, that the market puts a high value on a skilled person's time leads the individual to offer it more hours, that innovation is rapid leads a person to make the most of a skill or asset currently in high demand (it might not always be!). The majority of those caught up in the faster economic flow are under pressure – to meet deadlines, to perform, to be available, to grasp opportunities, to meet the rising expectations of their families, to compete. Some are 'on line' to their employers all the time, an ambiguous benefit of the mobile phone and the modem. A growing number are self-employed. More carry on at least part of their job from their homes. Their bank balances and/or assets are increasing, but they are under no illusion as to the effort this is costing them.

103. Some of the long hours worked may not be a matter of individual choice at all. Companies that face increasing competition can restructure in ways that work the cores of their existing workforces more intensively. Employees may not be told, but they will know, that unrestricted availability to the company better guarantees their place in it. It is only when individuals are older that they may feel that their savings and assets have reached a level where they are, at last, free to choose working fewer hours rather than more, and that being passed over for promotion or even leaving the company are now acceptable risks. By that time, however, their children may have been reared, and hobbies and interests outside of work been badly neglected.

104. **Children notice** how scarce their parents' time has become. Dual income households are increasing. Young families (households with children aged under 15) have become twice as likely to have both parents working as older families. Fathers of young children are just as likely as other men in employment to put in a long working week, with some weekday evenings, Saturdays and even Sundays frequently included.[100] This value put on market time and the consequent feeling of unremitting pressure are nowhere seen more clearly than in the surging demand for childcare facilities.[101] The 'cost'

56

of parenting appears to have risen in several senses. Mothers in the higher socio-economic groups can experience that the dynamics of a career and the dictates of being 'professional' tend to penalise a preference for part-time work, job-sharing, flexi-hours, or leaves of absence for family reasons. Mothers in low-skilled services employment can find that the toil of public transport between their job and home, with commuting sometimes made necessary twice a day by the staggered nature of their hours, increasingly saps the energy they bring to the work awaiting them in the home.[102] Many parents feel trapped between the demands of their careers and jobs and what they want for their children.

105. A time each day when the family sits together at table is disappearing from many homes. Several things appear to be conspiring to make the family meal unusual on weekdays, or even at all: the working hours of parents; the different lifestyles of family members; the growing range of electronic entertainments available at any hour. In this area, the injunction 'make time!' is an invitation to breathe new contentment into the home, to remind parents and children of how listening to each other and sharing some of the joys and disappointments of a day are more deeply satisfying than an additional hour of work squeezed in or passed before a television or play-station.

106. **The elderly notice** how scarce their grown-up children's time has become. Uniquely in the European Union, the proportion of the Irish population aged 65 or over will not begin to rise for some years yet. However, there will still be – in absolute numbers – more elderly people in Irish society over the coming years and, thanks to medical advances, they will be of a higher average age.[103] Many retired people enjoy good health and are actively involved in the mainstream of society, through their role as grandparents (including, at times, child-minding), their participation in active age groups, their involvement in parish and community organisations. Even for them, however, there is much in the faster moving Ireland that is difficult in a new way – increased traffic on the roads, more crowded public

transport, a heightened sense of vulnerability in the home and on the street. There is, also, a growing number of old people who have little social contact and live on their own without family or close friends nearby. Some even find the biblical blessing of 'length of days' a mixed one, and fear less they become 'a burden' on their busy children and grandchildren. The number of very elderly people in different types of residential care is increasing, and some find family visits become less frequent, more rushed, or die away altogether.

107. The greatest need of the very aged is for more human contact. Their presence in the lives of families and in communities is another quiet invitation to 'make time!' and to give it, not to earning or spending, but to enhancing directly the quality of life for them, but also for all who come to know them. Priority attention given the housebound by priests and other pastoral workers and the expansion of day-care centres are so many examples of responses promoting the social inclusion of the very old. Children, in particular, can benefit much from getting to know and love them. Irish society should aspire to 'a vital osmosis between the old and the young which liberates the first from solitude and abandonment, and which enriches the second with the wisdom that is proper to the ageing'.[104]

108. Time with loved ones, time to 'waste' on those who need us but can 'do' nothing for us, is squeezed not just by the pressures of work but, ironically, by the activity of spending as well. Advanced industrial societies tend, indeed, to bring more leisure hours for the majority of their populations, and this is frequently taken in the form of longer 'weekends'. As people's disposable income rises, strong leisure industries develop to help them use their time outside work for entertainment, sport, travel and cultural pursuits. Indeed, the widening range of consumer options targeting people's 'free time' can introduce a note of stress even into long weekends. The observation that someone 'works hard and plays hard' captures the sense in which, for some people, high consumption compensates for the discipline and effort of being a high-earner.

109. Weekday earning and weekend consumption, thus, alike make people aware that time is scarce. The **Christian Sunday** has always sought to do more than encourage rest from labour. It is essentially about savouring a non-instrumental relationship with the material world, a 'grateful adoration' of its Creator, and creating 'a time to see the true face of the people with whom we live'.[105] With the Eucharist at its heart, it fosters a quality to time, a moment when human beings together can accept that they are part of creation without having to use it, and acknowledge this before their Creator. They are able to 'contemplate' all that is, with themselves as part of it, and to display 'that disinterested, unselfish and aesthetic attitude that is born of wonder in the presence of being and of the beauty which enables (them) to see in visible things the message of the invisible God who created them' (*Centesimus Annus, 37*).

110. Leisure, in fact, can overwhelm the spirit of Sunday! 'When Sunday loses its fundamental meaning and becomes merely part of a "weekend", it can happen that people stay locked within a horizon so limited that they can no longer see the heavens'.[106] Never has it been more necessary and more difficult for people to make conscious decisions that create time for themselves, their families and friends, and their God. Many do, by making Sunday their particular day for 'wasting' time with their children, their parents, or for visiting those in hospital. The struggle to 'keep Sunday special' is, in fact, not centrally concerned with shop opening hours at all; it is about the spirit and practice of 'making time' in ways that give meaning to how time is used during the rest of the week. Time spent with God and the Christian community in Church, with those who need us and can have the quality of their lives enriched simply by our presence with them for a while, is, of course, not wasted. Rather, it makes our relationships and our whole life become more profoundly human.

111. In summary, a rapidly expanding economy can be a hard task master. As a greater proportion of the population begins to earn, and earn at higher levels, it is more necessary than ever that Christians give witness to their core perspective on work: it

is the person who gives her or his work its fundamental value, not the market (*Laborem Exercens,* 6). Christians remind themselves most forcefully of this truth when they make time for those people to whom the market attributes no value.

4.3   *More of everything, except security?*

112. The process of rapid economic growth appears, paradoxically, to increase the number of people who feel vulnerable. It challenges and dislocates many. It only happens, and is sustained, because ongoing adaptation and changes are accepted in more and more workplaces. New timetables, new procedures, new reporting structures, new products, new technologies, greater competition, the constant replacement of colleagues – all generate pressure and stress. A much greater flow of wealth is being made possible by a vastly greater input of human time, energy and inventiveness. The traffic congestion, the longer opening hours, the office lights burning later in the evening, are so many signs that society does not get more out of its economy without putting more in.

113. Even success in attaining a relatively good income does not guarantee freedom from this growth in insecurity. There is a heightened vulnerability to swings in share values and whatever might threaten the value of property. There is worry that children become accustomed to a lifestyle and place in society that they will have great difficulty in sustaining as independent adults. There may be worries about the tenure of employment, the flow of further contracts, the future of the company, and what competitors are doing. These factors can create stress even before considering the fall-out of social inequalities, family breakdown and addictions: the burglaries, muggings, vandalism, car theft, and growing unease on the streets. Some in Ireland today would have little difficulty agreeing with the Bible: 'a person's life is not made secure by what he owns, even when he has more than enough' (Lk 12:15).

114. A contributing factor to the growing sense of vulnerability is that, in fast-expanding urban areas, fewer people experience

the neighbourhood where they live as a community. The reasons underlying this are common to modern urban societies everywhere: greater mobility as people follow where the jobs are, or where the houses have been built; greater affluence and the motor-car making it possible to socialise and maintain friendships independently of where one is living; more affluence making lending or sharing between households unnecessary; greater caution as neighbours become increasingly unknown; a greater desire to be undisturbed at home as working life becomes more stressful and pressured; the greater reliance on electronic media in the home for entertainment and communication; more households without children and, thus, without the contacts children tend to generate between houses. The resulting degree of reliance on the nuclear family and individually constructed networks of friends works well for many, but not for all. Modern urban living features a surprising amount of loneliness.

115. It is not just the person with more to lose who can feel increasingly vulnerable, but people who are poor as well. The unrelenting demands being made on emergency centres make clear that individuals on society's lowest incomes are also experiencing life as more demanding and more pressured in these new economic times. Many of the low-skilled jobs available to them offer broken and difficult hours, often on short-term contracts; public transport times to work have increased; the expectations of their families too have risen sharply, while debt has never been easier or more tempting to enter into; the prospects of their older children getting a place in which to live have dramatically worsened, and drugs are more widely available, with horrendous consequences for their neighbourhoods. Frequently, those above them on the income ladder simply do not see, blinded by their own problems, weighed down by their own increased expectations.[107] Policies expressing solidarity, however, will only be formulated and find political support when more of the better-off in society *do* see, and when they accept that an economy that is moving faster is more demanding of people who are poor also, not more benign.

116. It is, arguably, becoming more difficult for those benefiting the most from economic growth to see what the same process is entailing for others. The environmental and social stresses caused by rapid economic growth make it more attractive for wealthy people to live in designer neighbourhoods, purchase all their schooling and medical care from private institutions, and, generally, arrange their social life and relaxation in ways that cut them off from the reality of the country of which they are a part. This effective withdrawal from the rest of society needs to be countered with persuasion and assurance. Success is good, the generation of wealth is good, and the successful and wealthy should not have to hide themselves away nor seek special protection. However, reliance on greater private resources rather than higher public standards to achieve pleasant neighbourhoods and security in socialising is surely misplaced. That is one lesson of societies more wealthy than that of Ireland.[108] As an example, everyone benefits when even people who own fine cars find it acceptable and efficient to use public transport.

117. In summary, growing private wealth in a society where solidarity and social love do not grow apace casts a pall on human togetherness. This can be seen in urban areas where walls between residential neighbourhoods with different socio-economic groups grow higher, pretty homes are festooned with burglar alarms, trip-switch lights and closed circuit video cameras, and pedestrians who stroll are regarded with suspicion. It can be seen in rural areas where beautiful homes, by the sea coast or overlooking inland waterways, on quayside or mountainside, remain empty for long stretches of time, and where trespass signs on fences and gates begin to multiply.

118. We state the Christian point of view, not just to those who purchase luxury homes in rich ghettos[109] but to all who would like to: 'Be suspicious of anything on your part that appears an attempt to lock yourselves away from the rest of society. You may try to do it, but you will end up contributing indirectly to a more polarised and less attractive society. Your own lifestyle and that of your children will begin to resemble that of tax exiles in an overseas country. But this is your country, and you

can do much better by way of making it a satisfying and wholesome place in which to live!'

4.4 *Rearing children well at a time when they are a key consumer market*

119. In homes of every income level, parents struggle to deal with the consequences of the fact that children have become a key consumer market. Much more so than adults, children lack the experience and independence of judgement to decide for themselves what they want, to distinguish want from need, and to know when enough is enough. Parents can be baffled at the power of a designer label to spell acceptance or rejection of a gift, joy or misery in the wearing of a garment. They can feel at a distinct disadvantage as their children take readily to new electronic entertainments, finding it difficult even to know what their children are doing, much less the long-term consequences of hours passed with play-stations, television and the internet. The steady appearance of new products, which children know their friends will find exciting, makes children increasingly avid for pocket money and, when they are old enough, for part-time work.

120. The level of consumer expenditure incurred on behalf of, and by, children is one of the most remarkable features distinguishing Irish society today from that of previous decades. The joy and pride of adults in giving, and the delight of children in having, needs to be balanced with other values and to reckon with the innate limitation of material things to fill even young hearts. Children need constant help to learn that other people have needs, and needs that, on occasion, must take priority over their own wants. They also need to be helped to see through the false promises of repeatedly changing consumer products, to find contentment in moderation, and to grow in understanding of their relative good fortune in a world as ill-divided as the present one. These are huge responsibilities on parents in today's social climate.

121. Advertising is frequently a force compounding the difficulties facing parents. The industry knows both that children have considerable purchasing power of their own and that, in many

homes, they have a large influence on their parents' consumption decisions. This is a major incentive to target children even though they have a limited ability to form judgements of their own. It is a good example of the EU working to raise standards that Sweden is considering using its first presidency of the Union to press for the extension to all Member States of its practice in banning television advertising targeted at children.

4.5   The Bible and wealth

122. The Bible teaches that individual wealth has, in fact, only a very limited ability to deliver on the things that most fill the human heart. It speaks of true friendship, being loved for who one is, a tranquil conscience, joy in giving as well as in receiving, replacing enmity with trust, and of other spiritual accomplishments, as making a person rich. Of course, most people accept this as true and yet, simultaneously, they feel more money is 'definitely' likely to help rather than get in the way of *their* greater happiness. However, as disposable income rises, so do human wants; it becomes more difficult to know and decide independently when the current standard of living is genuinely satisfactory. It is particularly difficult for the young. Older people, at least, can use their ability to have enjoyed life and friendships in former times when they had much less money as a reference point in the present, and smile at what younger people have come to regard as 'musts'.

123. The lives of a great number of people in the world, including a substantial minority within Ireland, would be utterly transformed by a modest increase in their material resources. From a Christian perspective, therefore, great personal wealth constitutes a mountain of opportunities. Christian baptism dissolves all boundaries in creating the family of the Church,[110] and the neighbour and friend of the Christian is whatever individual is in need (Lk 10:36-37). Not for nothing does Jesus make clear that holding onto, or seeking, great wealth for exclusive enjoyment is simply incompatible with Christian discipleship (Lk 16:13, 18:24-25, Mk 10:17-22).

124. What the Bible has to say can be summarised thus: wealth, a command over substantial material resources, gives its owners a greater chance to show their **inner** wealth and reveal who they really are. It is not so much that a large personal fortune, of itself, either brings happiness or causes misery in the biblical sense, but that the person who uses it in one way – metaphorically speaking, to build 'bridges' with others – is blessed or happy, while the person who uses it differently – to build 'walls' against others – is not. Those who retain serious wealth in today's world purely for their own enjoyment are forced by the Bible to realise that they are not responding to Lazarus at the gate (Lk 16) simply because *they do not want to.* In this sense, great financial wealth throws a harsh light on its owners; they might long to be a different type of person but, sadly, they see how in fact they are: 'the young man went away sad, for he was a man of great wealth' (Mt 19:22). As for all who are not particularly rich, the spirit of the Gospel invites them to feel grateful rather than disappointed. Which of us could be sure that, possessing serious wealth, we would prove any less determined to retain it, and any less creative of 'good' reasons as to why we should, even in a world as needy as our own.

125. Christians – every one of whom is called to be 'poor in spirit' (Mt 5:3) – should be a blessing in a society that wishes to be pro-active in fostering social inclusion. As followers of Jesus, we are able to experience what we earn and own, at the one time, as personal achievement and as gift. We experience a spiritual joy **in** material things because they are 'the fruit of the earth and the work of human hands', because they are God's gifts, of which we have the use but are not, in any absolute sense, the owners. We have met a generous God and want to be generous. Just as we delight in receiving and relish how good creation is, so we delight in sharing. We know no blessing from God is ever directed to us as isolated individuals but as persons with a capacity for enriching relationships. As we seek ways to share those resources for which we have responsibility, we actually experience the blessing of which Jesus speaks. We realise we are being made more fully alive, brought into a deeper and wider solidarity with others, and saved – in a real

sense – from being owned by our own possessions: 'Give, and there will be gifts for you: a full measure, pressed down, shaken together and overflowing, will be poured into your lap; because the standard you use will be the standard used for you' (Lk 6:38).

PART FIVE

Looking Forward

5.0 *The reasons for looking forward*

126. No one foresaw the scale of the economic boom in the 1990s; no one can guarantee that the decade 2000-2010 will bring only further advances. For example, the fractures beginning to widen in Irish society are capable of souring life for everyone, and materialism is capable of undermining people's ability to find contentment in what they already own. To counter such challenges effectively, key social and cultural values, which have been present to some extent in the transformation of the 1990s, must be strengthened and developed. They need to find expression in the further development of Ireland's solidarity with the poorest nations and in the forging of a stronger ethic of consumption, of work and of civic responsibility within Ireland. Only then will society make those choices that best serve the common good.

5.1 *Ireland's prosperity and poorer nations*

127. While Ireland enters the new millennium with justifiable confidence and pride, it is important that Irish people not lose sight of the extent to which, in a highly interdependent world, prosperity is as much a gift as a conquest. Above all, Irish society needs to be permeated with a lively awareness that, while the country is currently navigating the turbulent waters of international markets with success, other nations – much less well equipped than Ireland – are finding these same waters hostile, and some are in danger of sinking altogether. The poorer nations can and must also benefit from Ireland's improved stewardship of its economic resources. Some of the global changes needed in the interests of wider justice will impact on Ireland too; after all, some of the international markets that Ireland is skilfully using to its advantage are either closed to the poorest countries or pushing them deeper into poverty.[111] Massive and entrenched world poverty is the

single saddest legacy of the twentieth century to the new millennium.

128. The outside perspective on the Republic of Ireland has tended to be of a relatively poor society facing deep-rooted structural problems as it attempted to build a modern economy. The Irish people, however, were also seen to have a deep empathy with the efforts of poorer nations to develop, and with their struggle for a more just world economic order. The involvement of Irish NGOs and missionaries in that struggle, and the extent to which their work has rested on voluntary subscriptions from the public, constitute a proud chapter in contemporary Irish history. At the same time, Irish governments and interest groups lobbying in Brussels acquired the reputation for being tough negotiators and playing the cards of smallness and relative underdevelopment to maximum effect. Negotiating with the larger and more wealthy EU Member States never appeared the apposite time for acknowledging that the Common Agricultural Policy, from which some Irish farmers were doing extremely well, endangered small producers in impoverished nations, or that the return on Structural Funds' monies would be much higher in the six countries applying for EU membership (where the per capita income is only some 20 per cent of the EU average) than in Ireland.

129. The success of the 1990s and the good outlook for the Irish economy to the year 2010 constitute a huge opportunity to make solidarity with poorer nations an even stronger dimension of Irish life. Ireland's shoulders will be broader, and correspondingly more able to carry a larger share of efforts to promote a better world over the next decade. The vast majority of Irish people, we believe, do not want to live in a European oasis of prosperity surrounded by an impoverished world, much less to take part in constructing greater fortifications against it. On the contrary, they wish to help in creating a new culture of international solidarity and co-operation, where all – particularly the wealthy nations and the private sector – accept responsibility for an economic model which serves everyone.

130. Sustained economic growth will give Irish governments a greater ability to insist that the EU exemplify this new culture of international solidarity and co-operation. When the next round of negotiations takes place on the allocation of the Structural Funds (in 2006), it is with pride that Ireland should be present as a net contributor.[112] It would also be highly symbolic and enormously enhance Ireland's credibility and voice, if, by then, the UN target for official development assistance of 0.7 per cent of GNP had been attained.[113] Ireland's main contribution to forging a more just world economic order will always be qualitative rather than quantitative; even its vastly expanded economy remains insignificant in world terms. However, rather than thinking that this makes the level of what the country does give, and the promptness and efficiency of its responses, less important, every element of generosity and 'going the extra mile' by Ireland should be seen as increasing its leverage in EU and world affairs.

131. Irish governments will only do this, of course, in response to an informed and articulate public, speaking through its NGOs, Churches, trade unions and other intermediate organisations. It would be a tragedy if, during the very decade when it was feasible to reinforce and reimagine Irish policy in many key areas affecting relationships with the poorer world, Irish society were to lose interest in doing so. Greater official solidarity with poorer nations must not be partly offset by a fall in the high levels of voluntary commitment that characterised Irish society in much less fortunate times. The first decade of the new millennium offers Ireland the opportunity to develop a more mature relationship with the EU, viewing it no longer mainly as a source of support for Irish economic development, but as a privileged institutional set-up that magnifies the country's efforts to help cement peace and prosperity in Central and Eastern Europe, respond to global crises and forge a more just world economic order.[114] The traditionally high level of enthusiasm among the Irish 'for Europe' should not begin to weaken just because the net financial inflows are less.

132. The principal contribution Ireland makes to the EU and the wider world will continue to lie in the quality of its own society. To the extent that Ireland's integration into world markets and rapid adoption of new technologies does not lead more of its people to become personally obsessed with a higher material standard of living, despoil their environment, or tolerate wide social inequalities, nations poorer than Ireland will get a powerful example and encouragement to pursue their own better economic performance in ways that are also compatible with compassion, inclusiveness, global solidarity and environmental responsibility.

5.2 Major societal choices facing Ireland

133. Over the next decade, it will be the choices made by Irish people individually and collectively that will determine the overall quality of life on this island. Many strategic directions will be taken that, in effect, give expression to the collective commitment to the common good. For example:

- Have people dependent on social welfare a right to benefit from the overall growth in the economy to the extent that their incomes (old age and widow/er's pensions, disability and invalidity benefits, one-parent family allowance, unemployment assistance, etc.) should be linked to average earnings, or are modest increases slightly ahead of the cost of living the most that should be guaranteed to some groups among them?

- Should Ireland's recourse to taxation and public social expenditures remain relatively low and public social services accordingly be narrowly targeted (the 'Anglo-Saxon' model), or should the tax base be widened and improved public social services be made widely available without a large reliance on means-testing (the 'Continental European' model)?

- Is the all-important flexibility of the workforce (people's willingness to retrain, change tasks, switch jobs, etc.)

better achieved by exposing people to more of the consequences of not adapting, or by strengthening safety nets (income guarantees, workplace protection, etc.) under them as they undertake changes?

- Should social assistance be available indefinitely to individuals capable of work but not finding suitable jobs, as at present, or – after a certain period – should a specific service to the community be required of them and/or a publicly subsidised job be guaranteed?

- To what extent will company boards, professional associations, individuals and all who influence remuneration packages at the highest levels accept that there comes a time when the scale of the gap between the very wealthy and those at the bottom of the range of income begins to undermine the common good?

This Letter proffers no technical expertise to help decide these major societal choices. However, the value issues inherent to the choices passionately concern all Christians. Catholic social teaching grounds clear sympathies as to what the objectives should be, but it does not specify the concrete policies to be adopted as the means. Christians can validly differ as to which policies better serve the common good but will be united in urging a wider and deeper conversion to it in the first place.

5.3 *The time for imaginative and bold changes*

134. Christians are aware of the fragility of any human accomplishment. One result of becoming wealthier, as individuals and as a society, is that people steadily extend control over their lives and environment. Or they think that they do. For that is ever true only in a very limited sense. A person's 'standard of living' may appear to be stored up for years to come, as the promise latent in investments of different sorts, but, rich and poor, our individual lives – and our societies – always remain vulnerable to factors we cannot control (Lk 12:16-21).

135. Many Irish people are aware that the country's dependence on world peace, the stability of the global economic system and the health of the US economy has grown apace with its economic success.[115] However, too great an emphasis on what is vulnerable in Ireland's impressive economic performance could have the perverse effect of making individuals and groups want to do well 'while they can' and 'put aside' as much as possible. While the future is inherently unseen, there is a wide consensus that, over the next decade at least, Ireland – barring major mishaps – will continue to enjoy good economic growth, a continuing rise in the proportion of its population engaged in earning and higher disposable incomes. There has not been, since the foundation of the State, as favourable an immediate background or benign an economic outlook for setting ambitious social and environmental targets and achieving them.

5.4 The dignity of the human person

136. Ireland's new wealth as a country will only be reconciled with a genuinely higher quality of life for everyone on this island to the extent that Irish society is characterised by an energetic and widespread regard for the dignity of the human person. This dignity is inherent to every human being. It is not for any law to confer it, nor can any social circumstance or hazard of health remove it. Where political institutions or social conditions do not acknowledge it, it is *their* claim to legitimacy and acceptance that is accordingly reduced. The United Nations Universal Declaration of Human Rights in 1948 was a powerful embodiment of the growing human consciousness in this regard. The Christian faith nurtures, reinforces and illuminates this awareness that the dignity of the human person is the criterion by which every political, economic and social development is to be judged: 'people are the source, the focus and the aim of all economic and social life' (*Gaudium et Spes,* 63). While all creation bears the imprint of God, the human being alone is 'in the image of God' (Gn 1:27).

137. Pope John Paul II has developed this aspect of the Church's social teaching. At the start of his pontificate, he resolutely stated that 'the human person is the primary route that the Church must travel in fulfilling her mission' (*Redemptor Hominis*, 14).[116] That means that fidelity to her mission requires the Church to champion the cause of the human person in this age of prodigious technical accomplishments, population growth, concentration of power and entrenched socio-economic inequalities. In the face of each development, the Church's message is simple: 'Respect every human person! Each one is made in God's image'.[117] It is just this message that Irish society needs to take to its heart as it enters the new millennium.

138. Everything must be made to hinge around the dignity of the human person. Economic activity can, indeed, be brought to serve the good of the whole person and of every person (*Populorum Progressio*, 14), but if a society neglects the virtues of justice and charity, solidarity and compassion, respect for the integrity of creation and temperance, it is difficult to see how else it will. Each of these virtues should inform an ethic of consumption, an ethic of work and an ethic of civic responsibility.

5.5 *An ethic of consumption*

139. An 'ethic of consumption' is probably the least developed area of Church social teaching today. The status of being a consumer and the place accorded the activity of consuming in Western societies are without precedent in human history. Buying goods and services produced by the market is one of the most universal and bonding of all social activities engaged in by their populations, and one of the most socially divisive. On the one hand, anyone can stroll the malls of a new shopping centre, some to experience facilities that far surpass what they have in their own homes and neighbourhoods. On the other hand, the marketing and purchase of many goods and services is based expressly on their exclusivity: what one person purchases sets her or him apart from those who do not.

140. More Irish households are already enjoying purchasing power that is formidable by previous Irish, and current global, standards, and that power is predicted to rise substantially over the next ten years. One result is that additional consumer expenditures are no longer so automatically linked to securing basic improvements in living standards, such as a bed for each child, heating in the home, new clothing for all adults or an annual holiday. The distinction between needs and wants, basics and luxuries, is becoming more blurred in the expenditure patterns of Irish households. More of their consumer choices are free to revolve around the creation of lifestyles that accommodate 'the quest for truth, beauty, goodness and communion with others for the sake of common growth' (*Centesimus Annus*, 36). In that Encyclical Letter, Pope John Paul II also says: 'It is not wrong to want to live better; what is wrong is a style of life which is presumed to be better when it is directed towards "having" rather than "being", and which wants to have more, not in order to be more but in order to spend life in enjoyment as an end in itself' (36). In fact, as the market economy ceaselessly innovates and multiplies what it offers, it becomes increasingly difficult for anyone to decide independently what is enough.

141. Wide perspectives and determined policies are needed to give direction to consumption in a world that has become more interdependent and for an environment under increasing strain. As the United Nations' *Human Development Report 1998* states it: 'Consumption clearly contributes to human development when it enlarges the capabilities of people without adversely affecting the well-being of others, when it is as fair to future generations as to the present ones, when it respects the carrying capacity of the planet and when it encourages the emergence of lively and creative communities'.[118] Christians, in deciding on their lifestyles and distinguishing legitimate needs from frivolous wants, are called to consult the pervasiveness of poverty at home and abroad. They will feel deeply uneasy with any practice of conspicuous consumption when over one-fifth of the Irish population struggle to avoid social exclusion because of their lack of

resources, and a much greater percentage of the world's population is mired in poverty.

142. A larger population enjoying greater purchasing power can engage in several forms of inefficient or self-defeating expenditure patterns in pursuit of individual objectives which enlightened public measures could deliver more efficiently. For example, ease of circulation in a city centre or living in a quiet village become unattainable if very large numbers of people buy cars or houses in an effort to enjoy them. What is needed are people willing to choose improved public transport and support better local planning. Personal commitment to the common good will also influence the individual household's use of water and energy, generation of waste and level of co-operation with recycling. The more that people are willing to embrace changes to their own habits, and to co-operate with and support the public authorities in discharging their responsibilities in this area, the more likely it becomes that further economic growth will enhance the environment and not degrade it. In this area it is particularly true that 'how we spend our money is as important as how much we spend'.

143. Some of what is being spent out of the higher disposable incomes in Ireland today is clearly not enhancing anyone's capabilities, and adversely affecting the wellbeing of others. A prominent example is the abuse of alcohol, in particular on the part of young people. The different pressures on them are bringing heavy drinking to characterise younger and younger age groups, and this induces a terrible narrowing of their lives.[119] One hundred years ago, the Pioneer Total Abstinence Association was founded as a profound Christian response to a widespread abuse of alcohol, then largely as an anaesthetic for hardship. The irony and shame should not be lost on Irish society that, a century later, alcohol is again being abused – on the scale that it is – by people coping, this time, with the fruits and the pressures of economic success. The depth and extent of the suffering being caused individuals and families by alcohol abuse in Ireland make the National Alcohol Policy deserving of a much greater awareness and more forceful implementation.[120]

144. On the positive side, however, there are inspiring examples of where individuals as consumers seek to organise and use their purchasing power to improve the terms of trade with poorer countries, to improve working conditions for vulnerable groups of workers, to minimise damage and strain on the environment (promoting 'green' products, recycling, etc.), and to insist on higher ethical standards on the part of boards of directors. As material living standards climb in Ireland, it is to be hoped that Christian interest in and commitment to these forms of advocacy will grow in extent and in practical effectiveness. Personal responsibility always remains, in how we spend our money as in everything else.

5.6 *An ethic of work*

145. The increasing pervasiveness of markets steadily raises the prominence of consumption as an activity in the Western world. However, Church social teaching identifies the Western attitude to, and practice of, work as what must first change if the activity of consumption is to find its proper place.[121] Clearly, if the only motivation in working longer hours and earning more is to be able to spend more, invitations to a less consumer-oriented lifestyle and to voluntary restraint in how money is spent come too late.

146. Pope John Paul II spelt out the Christian understanding of work in *Laborem Exercens,* and his insights are more relevant than ever as Ireland nears full employment. Three merit particular attention:

- It is not work, much less earning a great deal of money, that confers value on an individual. Rather, it is the innate dignity of the human person that gives the work of each individual a value that is prior to what the market may recognise. People wanting to work, therefore, should not lightly be considered 'unemployable', and there should be suspicion of the valuation taking place when the emigration of unskilled Irish people is overlooked at a time when every effort is being made to attract skilled Irish and non-Irish workers from overseas.[122]

- People demean their own dignity when they measure the value of the work they do solely by the measuring stick of money. There are important and valuable forms of work that are not paid. There is also an obligation to exercise moderation in the hours devoted to earning in order to maintain health and allow personal development in and through the context of other relationships. A growing number of children in Ireland are entitled to question the dominance their parents give to earning.

- The work a person does and the human dignity of that person are indissociable. Thus, neither an employer nor a country can just take an individual's hours of labour and no more; they must also assume some responsibility for the worker's overall wellbeing and integration into society. This includes especially the under-eighteen-year-olds and the immigrants who are being brought into the Irish workforce in larger numbers.

147. There is a growing consensus that remaining 'employable' is the more appropriate objective for the individual today rather than a 'job for life'. If this is what society expects of the individual, then it is important that it correspondingly supports 'life-long learning', including in the workplace, and makes moving in and out of job-holding as easy as possible.[123] Anecdotal evidence suggests that some people (mostly in the private sector) are being asked to shoulder extreme levels of 'flexibility' (such as almost wholly unstructured working hours or zero security in their employment) while, at the other extreme, others are exacting undue compensation for allowing innovations that, in effect, improve their working conditions. Solidarity between all those in the workforce may be at its weakest in this regard.

148. Well before the economic boom, the family in Ireland was under pressure, principally from a decline in the practice and stability of marriage. For example, the proportion of all births taking place outside marriage and the percentage of families with one parent have each been steadily increasing.[124] Into this context, the economic boom has brought new tensions arising from difficulties in reconciling work and family life. By 1997, 42 per cent of all mothers were participating in the workforce and for those with dependent children the rate was even higher (49 per cent). In fact, the evidence shows that parents with young children (under 15) are more likely to be in *full-time* employment than other categories of men and women.[125] This may be one reason why, even though women's overall employment rate in Ireland remains below the EU average, there is already a severe shortage of childcare facilities.[126]

149. The need to respond more effectively to the difficulties that mothers and fathers are experiencing in balancing the demands of their jobs with their parenting roles is one of the key issues facing Ireland over the coming decade. In a short time, Irish society has come a long way from a grudging acceptance that women should be entering the labour force during a period when unemployment was high, to realising that this was always going to be the consequence of wider and better education. In place of discriminatory arguments that 'the mother's place is in the home' (with its implication 'and only there'), the fairer argument is now advanced that 'each parent has a place in the home' (implying, this time, 'without prejudice to the role of each in the economy and wider society'). A great deal more is now known about the importance of active parenting *by the father,* for the good of children, for the mother who is freed to carry out roles outside the home at less cost to herself, for the father himself whose own life experience is enriched, and for the health and stability of the family unit itself.[127]

150. The childcare crisis, therefore, is much deeper than the economic issue of how employers can access the skills of people whom parenting responsibilities are making unavailable. It touches on values fundamental to society, the value put on children and the health of family life. Expert recommendations are at hand as to the different ways responsibility can be allocated between the modern welfare state itself, the private sector and voluntary organisations.[128] Resolute policy decisions are needed that fully acknowledge the *social* importance of what parents do as they rear their children. The case appears overwhelming for the payment of much greater child benefit, which could be taxable in the normal way, as one way of ensuring that the parent who chooses to stay at home is not overlooked by measures thought out largely from the vantage-point of the parent in employment.

151. Widening access to employment has been a wonderful feature of the 1990s, but wider options for people in how they do their jobs must characterise the next decade. For example, the option of part-time employment could play a greater role in facilitating many parents than at present. The contrast with the Netherlands is striking: 10 per cent more Dutch women hold a job than do Irish women, yet twice as many Irish women work full-time. A major reason is that the practice of part-time working is much more widespread in the Netherlands, among men as well; over three times as many Dutch men work part-time as Irish males.[129] Research has shown that the take-up of job-sharing, career breaks and flexible working-time arrangements is low in Ireland, and largely availed of by women where it happens.[130] Employers' practices and State policies undoubtedly have a huge role here in making family-friendly working arrangements more widespread and more attractive. Parents will not be slow to seize the opportunities presented by new policies to secure a balance between earning and caring for their children, such that their family life is never the casualty of their need or desire for higher incomes.

152. For some workers, their responsibilities in the home centre on the care of an elderly person or of a family member with a

disability. The needs of these workers are justly recognised as an integral part of the search for family-friendly working arrangements. Great social good results from public policies and workplace arrangements that allow carers also to work outside the home without the people depending on them being deprived of the attention they need. The Irish population aged 80 years or more will rise steadily in the first decades of the new century.[131] The type of thinking and policy responses being prompted by the childcare crisis of today could usefully be applied to the situation of many carers also. Innovative steps now could help ensure that an eldercare crisis does not develop at a future date.

...and the low-skilled

153. The economic boom has ushered Ireland faster down the road to the knowledge-based society and the services economy. These key characteristics of 'service' and 'knowledge' must be imbued with ethical content if employment of every sort is to remain the expression of a meaningful bond with others and of a contribution to the common good. The expanding services sector in innovating, trading economies today tends to feature a widening gap between the earnings of those whose know-how begins to command a global premium and those doing tasks that can be performed by any number of different types of worker (for example, immigrants, students, secondary earners). Yet, the simplest service is still one person doing something for another, and the highest-level consultation is still sharing human knowledge to the benefit of others.

154. As the Irish economy powers ahead, there must come a point at which the scale of the gap between the earnings of those with the scarcest skills and of those with the skills most plentifully available begins to undermine partnership in the workplace and the common good. The level at which people are paid is of public concern for two reasons. First, some people's best work may attract a wage so low that even their full-time work does not bring them a decent income.[132] Second, the total earnings of the highest paid may be so large

that they effectively undermine mutual respect in the wider workplace. Catholic social teaching is clear on the ideal: the conscientious contribution of every worker in the economy should be remunerated at a level that allows the individual to feel a valued colleague at what is a common workbench. 'Every human being sharing in the production process, even if he or she is only doing the kind of work for which no special training or qualifications are required, is the real efficient subject in this production process, while the whole collection of instruments…are only a mere instrument subordinate to human labour' (*Laborem Exercens,* 12).

155. The level of remuneration, therefore, must be neither so low nor so high that the relationship between people – their common humanity and equal dignity – is effectively belied. There is great symbolic and practical significance to the statutory national minimum wage. However, there is also a need for wider debate on the appropriate taxation of the accumulation of wealth and of earnings at the top end of the scale. It is morally unacceptable that those capable of commanding the highest earnings should consult only 'the going rate', as set by increasingly global markets, and not also the harmony of the society of which they are a part, and the moral obligations of the common good, in determining the level of remuneration for which they are willing to give of their best. The expanding Irish economy, while its dynamism is derived from high-skill, high-output sectors, still needs a significant number of people to perform relatively simple tasks. Energy and imagination should be invested in seeking to make these jobs satisfactory to more of the still numerous unemployed.

156. The Task Force on Long-Term Unemployment, employers and others have accepted that there are workers whom economic restructuring and recession have dealt with harshly and for whom it is wholly appropriate that society should take the responsibility of ensuring some type of sponsored employment. Christians will welcome this as a form of support that respects the dignity of people's work and their need to

contribute to society as well as receive from it. While every individual has a right to the minimum income needed for a dignified human life in society, the Christian is concerned that it reach the person in a way and a manner that increases their self-respect and willingness to contribute to society rather than undermining them.[133]

157. This observation of the Irish trade union movement merits wide consideration: 'With person-to-person services accounting for a growing proportion of new jobs, it is necessary to re-think the economic and social value of so-called "low-skilled" jobs. The current emphasis on quality of services as a vital competitive factor makes the person who serves the customer, cleans the toilet or answers the phone a key player on today's successful team. These service jobs require important and demanding attributes like inter-personal skills and commitment to consistent excellence in apparently menial or routine work. …There are no menial jobs in a high quality, high output economy'.[134]

…and immigrants

158. Immigrants are in a different position to refugees and asylum-seekers. Their motivation in coming to Ireland is simply to seek work that is better paid and/or a greater enhancement of their skills than they can find in their own country. The growing strength of the Irish economy in a global context will inevitably see an increase in the number of relatively low-skilled immigrants working in it. Given that so many Irish were in a similar position in other economies in former times, Ireland should aspire to the highest standards in this area. The legal immigrant taken on legally by an Irish employer should experience the same respect accorded to any worker in the economy. The level of their skills, their command of English, their unfamiliarity with Irish culture, their colour, religion, ethnic identity or nationality, nothing about them should be allowed to detract from their rightful place in Ireland and the dignity of their work. Nor should any downturn in economic activity be visited disproportionately on them. Employers need

to be pro-active in ensuring best practice is developed and adhered to, and full co-operation achieved with all the statutory and voluntary associations whose activities are also relevant to ensuring their foreign workers find living in Ireland satisfactory. The biblical injunction should have a particular ring in Irish ears: 'be mindful of the stranger in your midst! You were a stranger once, in the land of Egypt' (Lv 19:34).

...and which permeates the public sector

159. The implications of cash alone being the reason why a job is done and the loss of any sense of vocation are nowhere more potentially damaging than in the public sector. The ethos of public service, in the public sector and especially in national and local government, is an important **public asset**. Ireland in the future will be the poorer if its public sector does not continue to attract workers of the highest calibre, or if the attraction in question should no longer include pride that one is serving people on the basis of their need alone and enhancing the meaning of citizenship for everyone. The determination of public pay is deservedly considered a major issue needing resolution in the near future. Public perceptions that public services cost more than equivalent services in the private sector need frank examination and appraisal. While there is a widespread desire for improved public services in several areas, there is not always the corresponding willingness to support the public expenditure that would make this possible.

160. However, there should be nothing about the public sector that makes introducing new services and upgrading existing ones, in response to technological advances, more unlikely to happen, or more costly, than socially responsible employers are able to achieve in the private sector. The Government as employer and the public sector unions are engaging in an issue of huge import for the common good as they seek together to change pay relativities and work practices in a way that allows all *citizens* to benefit from new advances in product and service provision.

161. Nothing damages public confidence in, and support for, the public sector so much as instances of strike action where the disruption to the general public (in fact, frequently not the 'general' but the more vulnerable public) appears wholly disproportionate to the injury alleged or gains sought. Catholic social teaching has consistently upheld the right to strike but always on clear moral grounds and never just for expediency. The *moral* justification requires a clear 'yes' to each of four questions: 'Is it sure that real injustice is present? Is this injustice grave enough to justify the loss and the damage likely to be caused? Is there a proper proportion between the loss about to be inflicted and the lawful end pursued? Have all efforts been made to reach settlement by negotiation, and have these efforts failed?'[135]

162. The fact that a service is provided out of taxation to citizens, rather than purchased in the market by consumers, is no reason for the personnel involved to be underpaid or presumed on in any way. An eloquent example is public health services. No one wishes nurses, doctors or other healthcare workers to be taken advantage of and paid less than they deserve because, money apart, they are deeply dedicated to what they do. At the same time, few would like to think that services that can directly mean life or death, a full life or a diminished one, to potentially anyone, were being provided by people whose dominant interest in their work was money. This dilemma, keenly felt in the health services, illustrates a need throughout Irish society to restate and honour in practice that it is service to people which gives each job its true value and which payment acknowledges rather than confers.

5.7 An ethic of civic responsibility

163. This Letter seeks to help protect and improve the quality of everyone's life in Ireland as the country adjusts to unprecedented economic wealth. A long-term concern is that the hugely different valuations put on people by the international markets in which Ireland is now earning its living should not undermine the social and civic bonds that are

between them. A short-term concern is that responses to the revelations of different inquiries should not make partnership and solidarity more difficult to maintain and develop in the new decade. It is, therefore, on the theme of citizenship and civic culture that the Letter ends.

164. Public forums of inquiry have given many in Ireland a disillusioning insight into hidden corners of business and political life in the recent past. There is dismay at how the smallness of Irish society was taken advantage of by individuals in business, politics and the public service to create privileged circles, and revulsion at the elaborate efforts undertaken by some to conceal their financial transactions. There is disbelief at the scale of tax evasion practised by relatively well-off people at a time of acute national difficulties. There is anger at the indifference and contempt shown for public procedures and the common good by relatively fortunate individuals, and at how their selfish actions made the sacrifices of other sections of the community all the more burdensome.

165. It would be a great pity if the revelations of the inquiries were to fuel cynicism towards political life, create antipathy towards business success, weaken the ethos of public service, undermine the spirit of partnership, or renew an ambiguous attitude towards the payment of tax. The calibre of people who enter politics, business and the public service, and the development of a more tax-compliant culture, remain as critical to ensuring economic wealth serves the common good as they were to the generation of the boom in the first place. It is important, therefore, that no 'sides' are taken, and no generalised positions adopted, other than those in favour of the values that Irish society desires, and urgently wants, to have enshrined in the conduct of all its affairs – business, political, ecclesiastical and every other type. Those values are transparency, honesty, fairness, accountability, and respect for the common good. It is firmly to be expected that the sub-cultures the inquiries have uncovered belong wholly to the Ireland of yesterday, just as the vigour and impartiality of the inquiries reflect the Ireland of today. Ethical guidelines and

registers of interest are becoming the norm in politics and business, and individual behaviour is being challenged in areas and professions hitherto considered beyond criticism. This is to be welcomed. While respecting the need for utter thoroughness and fairness in the work of the different inquiries, the more quickly and firmly contemporary Ireland names and rejects deception and misdemeanours, and where necessary punishes criminal behaviour, the stronger the moral climate of today will become.

166. Our consultations during the preparation of this Letter left us in no doubt that people are concerned about a quality of life that higher disposable income alone cannot buy. Most Irish people want to live and see children reared in a country where there is a profound respect for each individual as a citizen, a respect that is real not just before the law but expressed in the standards of education, healthcare, income-support and housing that are available to those who are least well-off. Ireland's new economic circumstances require its society to clarify whether high standards in these areas are to be guaranteed universally to all members as citizens, through efficient and properly resourced public services funded out of taxation. Or is a two-tier system to be allowed develop further, with citizenship guaranteeing only a floor to standards in each area, while people are encouraged to purchase much higher standards for themselves out of their own incomes? In this context, the debate as to whether and how the Irish Constitution should enshrine a range of social and economic rights is one of great importance and deserves the widest possible participation.[136]

167. There is a growing individualism and competitiveness in Irish society and, in some quarters at least, a resistance to increased taxation to fund the maintenance and improvement of public services. Yet many people do support the public provision of better social services, not because of self-interest, but out of a conviction that all Irish children, no matter the circumstances of their birth, should have a minimum set of **opportunities** open to them to develop themselves, acquire the foundations

for a satisfying life and make their individual contributions to society. It was also our experience that many people support those public interventions that lessen inequalities in **outcomes** (in terms of income and wealth) because of their conviction that no social circumstance should deny the dignity of an individual human being.

168. By international standards, people in Ireland were paying the highest tax rate at relatively modest income levels even after the economic boom had transformed the state of the public finances. Equity and efficiency questions about how the current level of tax revenue is being raised, however, should not be allowed to hide the fact that, by the standards of other small, prosperous European societies, Ireland has low overall taxation and correspondingly low public social expenditures.[137] It is quite consistent to argue at the same time for lower tax rates on modest personal incomes *and* better public services, if the tax base is appropriately widened. The key moral issue for the individual is whether there is any type of extra taxation (for example, on property or energy use) or foregone tax reduction he or she will accept in order to support the State in raising the levels of healthcare, educational attainment, income protection and housing provision associated with Irish citizenship *per se*.

169. The Pensions Board broke welcome new ground in expressing the basic old-age pension it recommended the State should guarantee as a percentage of average industrial earnings; it proposed 34 per cent.[138] Some similar indexing of all social welfare payments to the growth of average earnings has yet to find widespread acceptance. Christians find it morally indefensible to maintain a financial incentive to work, which is appropriate and important in many instances, at the expense of a higher poverty risk being run by recipients of, for example, unemployment assistance and supplementary welfare allowances. It is, also, a minimalist form of solidarity when only minor real increases are granted to social welfare beneficiaries at a time when the average earnings in society are rising steadily.

170. The more developed civic responsibility needed to balance greater economic wealth must include environmental sensitivity as well as social solidarity. Concern for the environment is not synonymous with protection of the *status quo* but entails sharing and shaping the physical and natural environments in ways that benefit more people. Irish people must support measures designed to attain collectively what cannot be attained individually, for example, the extension and improvement of public transport systems, the attainment of EU standards in the treatment of waste water and the disposal of solid waste, the restriction of greenhouse gas emissions, the purity of inland water systems and coastal waters, the protection of wildlife habitats and the conservation of cultural and historical sites and buildings. This list, still not complete, is sufficient to highlight the extent to which Irish society must increasingly look to enlightened public policies if the current generation is to guarantee to the next what, in previous decades, was largely taken for granted – being able to find somewhere to live, finding a seat on a train, ease in disposing of household waste, quiet country lanes, fish in the lakes and rivers.

171. The more Irish people take part in helping decide the major societal issues facing the country, the greater is the prospect that the paths taken will, indeed, translate increased wealth into a widely-shared prosperity. There are some worrying signs that Ireland's civic culture may be weakening rather than strengthening. The percentage of the population exercising their right to vote in national elections has been steadily declining; voting turn-outs in socially disadvantaged areas are particularly low, compounding the danger that their needs receive low priority.[139] The percentage of employees in unions is some 48 per cent, but recent research shows that the large majority (69 per cent) describe themselves as 'rarely' involved, while one-half of those eligible to join unions have not done so.[140] Voluntary organisations of practically every sort are experiencing increasing difficulties in retaining and attracting volunteers.

172. The Christian perspective is clear. Voting responsibly is a practical embodiment of a commitment to the common good. Active participation in a union is a time-honoured way of showing effective solidarity not just with work colleagues but with all who are in danger of being marginalised from, or abused within, the world of work. Shareholding in a company is an opportunity to understand and influence that company's activities. Time given to parish, community and voluntary organisations can be a direct contribution to deepening the quality of life for others (and for oneself). The Christian response to low standards in any walk of public life is to take a more active part in helping restore integrity and transparency in serving the common good, and not withdrawal into a private, personal sphere. In preparing this Letter, we came into contact with wide and strong expectations of the good that Ireland's increased economic resources could do; we end it by pointing out that, in realising those expectations, each and every Christian has a role to play.

173. When we view the opportunities arising in Irish society because of rapid economic growth, and even more when we look at the island's living standards in their global context, we are in no doubt that this is a wonderful time to be a Christian. Wealth is an enormous latent power for doing good in a world as needy as our own. Divine revelation helps us see that either wealth is shared, or its owners become the owned and are diminished in themselves. This is a message that is liberating for rich and poor alike, each of whom is invited to see through the falseness of making material possessions the goal of human life and to experience the joy that the Spirit of God gives in the act of sharing. The Eucharist daily reminds us that creation is a shared table to which God has invited all of us equally. Each time we go out from Mass we are committed anew to transforming the experience of life for each person on the planet into a delighted surprise at the bounty and goodness of God.

1. For example: 'The Irish economy has notched up five straight years of stunning economic performance. No other OECD member country has been able to match its outstanding outcomes in a variety of dimensions' – the opening sentence in OECD (1999), *OECD Economic Surveys, 1998-1999: Ireland.*

2. OECD (1999).

3. Lev 25:1-55; Lk 4:18-19. Pope John Paul II, *Tertio Millennio Adveniente* (Preparation for the Jubilee of the Year 2000), 10 November 1994, especially 12 and 13.

4. Based on the real GDP growth rates for 1994-1999 given in Annex, Table 1, of OECD (1998), *OECD Economic Outlook,* December 1998. The distinction between Gross Domestic Product (GDP) and Gross National Product (GNP) is important for Ireland. GDP figures are used here because they measure the level of economic activity taking place within the State, which is what people most directly observe and impacts on the environment. GNP measures the level of economic activity for which Irish factors of production are responsible and, accordingly, tracks better the level of Irish incomes.

5. Over the period 1986-1996, cumulative employment grew by 26 per cent in Ireland, as against 15 per cent for the US. See J. Bradley, J. Fitz Gerald, P. Honohan and I. Kearney (1997), 'Interpreting the Recent Irish Growth Experience', *Medium-Term Review: 1997-2003.* For the second observation, see OECD (1999).

6. For example, 'Interpreting the Recent Irish Growth Performance', in J. Fitz Gerald, I. Kearney, E. Morgenroth and D. Smyth, eds. (1999), *National Investment Priorities for the Period 2000-2006,* pp. 29-42; F. Barry, ed. (1999), *Understanding Ireland's Economic Growth;* P. Tansey (1998), *Ireland at Work: Economic Growth and the Labour Market;* A. Gray, ed. (1997), *International Perspectives on the Irish Economy;* Bradley *et al.* (1997).

7. *Programme for National Recovery* (1987); *Programme for Economic and Social Progress* (1991); *Programme for Competitiveness and Work* (1994); *Partnership 2000 for Inclusion, Employment and Competitiveness* (1996). Interesting reflections by individual participants are in B. Reynolds and S. Healy, eds. (1999), *Social Partnership in a New Century.*

8. R. D. Putnam, R. Leonardi and R.Y. Nanett (1994), *Making Democracy Work: Civic Traditions in Modern Italy;* Jean-Philippe Platteau (1994), 'Behind the Market Stage where Real Societies Exist', *Journal of Development Studies,* Vol. 30, Parts I and II; D. C. North (1990), *Institutions, Institutional Change and Economic Performance.*

9. Pope John Paul II, *Centesimus Annus* (The Hundredth Anniversary), 1 May 1991.

10. Some of the programmes to which this paragraph refers include: the Local Drugs Task Forces in disadvantaged urban areas, the Integrated Services Project of Government departments and statutory agencies with responsibilities in disadvantaged areas, the Back to Work Allowance Scheme and similar programmes that dovetail social support with the taking of employment, the Fast Track in Information Technology (FIT) initiative which is opening up careers in the IT industry to people who are long-term unemployed, and the holistic approach to urban regeneration that characterises the Integrated Area Plans (IAP) of local authorities.

11. This is usually termed the 'productivity' of labour; it has improved steadily since the early 1960s.

12. See Fitz Gerald *et al.* (1999), especially figure 2.7.

13. Proceedings of 1971 Kilkenny Conference on Poverty, *Social Studies*, Vol. 1, No. 4, August 1972; L. Joyce and A. Mc Cashin, compilers (1981), *Poverty and Social Policy;* B. Harvey (1994), *Combating Exclusion: Lessons from the Third EU Poverty Programme in Ireland 1989-1994;* B. Nolan and C. T. Whelan (1994), Resources, Deprivation and Poverty.

14. *Centesimus Annus,* 34, 40, 42, 48. See also The Irish Episcopal Conference (1992), *Work is the Key,* paras. 72-74.

15. The Second Vatican Council, *Gaudium et Spes* (Pastoral Constitution on the Church in the Modern World), 7 December 1965. See also 26.

16. Pope John XXIII, *Pacem in Terris* (Peace on Earth), 11 April 1963.

17. For example, for the USA, see E. S. Phelps (1997), *Rewarding Work,* and R. Reich (1991), *The Work of Nations.* For the UK, see R. Marris (1996), *How to Save the Underclass.*

18. *The Common Good and the Catholic Church's Social Teaching* (1996), a Statement by the Catholic Bishops' Conference of England and Wales, para. 75.

19. Pope John Paul II, *Sollicitudo Rei Socialis* (The Social Concern of the Church), 30 December 1987. 'Sacred Scripture continually speaks to us of an active commitment to our neighbour and demands of us a shared responsibility for all of humanity. This duty is not limited to one's own family, nation or State, but extends progressively to all human kind, since no one can consider her or himself extraneous or indifferent to the lot of another member of the human family' (*Centesimus Annus,* 51).

20. *Strategic Planning Guidelines for the Greater Dublin Area,* 1999.

21. Peter Bacon & Associates, *An Economic Assessment of Recent House Price Developments,* April 1998; and *The Housing Market: An Economic Review and Assessment,* March 1999.

22. Dresdner Kleinwort Benson (1999), *Report on House Prices.*

23. Peter Bacon & Associates (1998), p. vi.
24. This was noted as a clear violation of Christian social teaching in *Work is the Key,* (1992), para. 60.
25. Manual workers accounted for 33.8 per cent of those securing loans from mortgage lending agencies in 1994, but for only 23.3 per cent in 1998; unskilled manual workers fared particularly badly, with their share falling from 7.3 per cent of loans to 3.4 per cent ('Analysis of Loan Approvals – Occupation of Borrowers', Department of the Environment and Local Government (1999), *Annual Housing Statistics Bulletin 1998,* p. 32).
26. The number of households on local authority waiting lists around the country increased by 43 per cent between March 1996 and March 1999, to reach over 39,000 (Dáil question time, 5 October 1999). An assessment of homelessness in Dublin, Wicklow and Kildare alone identified 2,900 homeless adults in the last week of March 1999 (J. Williams and M. O'Connor, 1999, *Counted In*). Current expenditure by health boards on the payment of rent and mortgage supplements as Supplementary Welfare Allowances was estimated to have risen by 113 per cent in five years (from £54m in 1994 to £115m in 1999); on average, in any one month of 1998, some 42,000 households in private rented accommodation and 8,000 with mortgages were being helped by SWA to meet their housing costs (Fitz Gerald *et al.,* 1999).
27. On youth homelessness, see P. McVerry SJ (1999), 'Twenty-Five Years of Homelessness', *Working Notes,* Issue 35.
28. Voluntary organisations such as the Society of St Vincent de Paul, Threshold, Simon Community, Sonas and Focus Ireland are deeply aware of the deteriorating situation of those vulnerable groups who have always had to rely on the private rented sector, for example, young families on housing lists, ex-prisoners, hostel users trying to resettle, refugees, women resettling after fleeing domestic violence, unemployed people, and older people, especially older women. They have made a joint submission to Government (June 1999) with detailed proposals for rent controls and security of tenure.
29. 'The assumption that public housing is provided by a reluctant administration to accommodate merely the homeless or those made so by development' contrasts strongly with many other European countries 'where it is treated as a public good with a much wider availability and function.' (J. A. Jackson and T. Haase, 1996, 'Demography and the Distribution of Deprivation in Rural Ireland' in Curtin *et al.,* p. 79). 'Local authority housing in Ireland is residualised to an extreme degree by European standards. It is now … at less than 9 per cent of the total housing stock, compared to a range of 15 to 30 per cent in most of the rest of western Europe.' (T. Fahey, ed., 1999, *Social Housing in Ireland: A Study of Success, Failure and Lessons Learned,* p. 235.)

30. 'The voluntary sector contributes less in Ireland than in many other countries to the housing of marginal groups such as people living in poverty and vulnerable old people.' (E. O'Shea, 1996, 'Rural Poverty and Social Services Provision', in Curtin *et al.*, p. 235.)

31. A provision in the Planning and Development Bill, 1999, published for discussion on 25 August 1999, by the Minister for the Environment and Local Government. The scope and type of provisions in this Bill are an example of the leadership that Ireland's new circumstances require; it is to be hoped that it will get a wide and fair hearing. The Society of St Vincent de Paul recommends that 15 per cent of all new private housing schemes should be made available to people on local authority waiting lists; see Society of Saint Vincent de Paul (1999), *Housing Policy: Mixed Housing and Mixed Communities.*

32. Department of the Environment and Local Government (1997), *Sustainable Development – A Strategy for Ireland;* Department of the Environment and Local Government (1998), *Circular Letter P/98 Residential Density.* Also Bacon (1998), section 43, p. xii; Bacon (1999), section 19, p. 5.

33. See Society of Saint Vincent de Paul (1999).

34. For example, when Ireland signed a global agreement on slowing the increase in greenhouse gas emissions (Kyoto, 1997), it did not seem that it would require major policy interventions to honour the commitment to hold the increase in Irish emissions to 13 per cent above their 1990 level by around the year 2010. Only two years later, the economic outlook had so changed that one estimate was that, without new policies, the outcome would be 32 per cent higher. Unlike in other countries, agriculture and not industry is the biggest single source of Ireland's 'global warming potential'. However, another land use, forestry, is the best single answer: the growth of forests ('carbon dioxide sinks') alone is thought capable of bringing down the estimated increase in emissions to 23 per cent. See Fitz Gerald *et al.* (1999).

35. This theme is returned to in discussing the need for an ethic of consumption (see section 5.5).

36. B. Nolan and T. Callan (1994), *Poverty and Policy;* B. Nolan and C. T. Whelan (1996), *Resources, Deprivation and Poverty.* The measure of 'consistent poverty' was adopted by the National Anti-Poverty Strategy in 1997. It is obtained by combining a low relative income (in this case, where people must live on a disposable income less than 60 per cent of the national average in a given year) with evidence of basic deprivation (the enforced absence, due to insufficient money, of food, clothing, heating, etc.).

37. The annual unemployment rate averaged over 15 per cent between 1987

and 1993. See also 'Poverty Trends – 1973 to 1994', in *Sharing in Progress: National Anti-Poverty Strategy* (1997), section 3.4.

38. T. Callan *et al.* (1999), *Monitoring Trends in Poverty for the National Anti-Poverty Strategy*, Final Report.

39. OECD (1999), Table 1.

40. The United Nations' Development Programme (UNDP), *Human Development Report 1998*, first developed and applied a 'human poverty index' tailored for industrial countries. Principally because of the weights this index gives functional illiteracy and long-term unemployment, Ireland ranked near the bottom of seventeen industrial countries for which data are compared, (Table 1.2, p. 20).

41. A. Barrett, T. Callan and B. Nolan (1999), 'Rising Wage Inequality, Returns to Education and Labour Market Institutions: Evidence from Ireland', *British Journal of Industrial Relations*, 37:1. P. Gottschalk and T. Smeeding (1997), 'Cross-National Comparisons of Earnings and Income Inequality', *Journal of Economic Literature*, Vol. XXXV.

42. ILO (1999), *Social Dialogue and Employment Success: Europe's Employment Revival – Four Small European Countries Compared*.

43. *The Work of Justice* (1977) called for a national programme to eliminate poverty. It was a time of economic recession but it argued that tackling poverty 'should not be postponed until our economic circumstances improve' (para. 102). The Justice Commission of the Conference of Religious of Ireland (CORI) , in particular, has consistently kept the unresolved issue of poverty alive in the public consciousness and as an issue for Government.

44. A major review of progress made in meeting commitments will take place at a special session of the UN General Assembly in Geneva in June 2000. Prior to that, the Council of Europe will be reviewing Europe's progress separately.

45. A significant number of people who are long-term unemployed cease to be classified as such because of their actual or recent participation on the Community Employment programme.

46. This is particularly evident when older and younger women are compared: half of all women reaching 65 and retiring in the late 1990s had only a primary education and less than one in ten a third-level qualification. By contrast, 6 per cent of women aged 25-29 had only a primary education and 35 per cent had completed third level (Fitz Gerald *et al.*, 1999, p. 60).

47. See *Human Development Report 1998*, which used the results of the first International Adult Literacy Survey co-ordinated by the OECD. A report by the UK's Basic Skills Agency placed Ireland second from the bottom, after Poland, in a study of basic adult literacy and numeracy skills. As it expressed it, one in five Irish adults could not use the index of a *Yellow*

Pages directory, and one in four, given money to buy a simple list of shopping, could not work out how much change they should receive.

48. B. Nolan *et al.* (1994), *Poverty and Time: Perspectives on the Dynamics of Poverty.*

49. 'Just as the British government declared the Great Famine over at the first sign of a potato crop, our government seems to have declared that we have recovered from unemployment because of a few excellent years of jobs growth. Heroin and crack cocaine have swept in behind the job famine, in the same way that cholera swept in behind the potato blight, decimating communities weakened by unemployment and despair. It isn't over.' M. Allen (1998), *The Bitter Word*, p. 51.

50. European Social Fund, Programme Evaluation Unit (1998), *ESF and the Long Term Unemployed;* P. O'Connell and F. McGinnitty (1997), *Working Schemes: Active Labour Market Policy in Ireland.* In the latter, the authors argue that what has been happening is 'perverse': 'those most in need of assistance are concentrated in the less effective programmes'.

51. An Action Plan for the Long-Term Unemployed from the State training agency, FÁS, commits it to raising the numbers of long-term unemployed people on its mainline training programmes from the low 11 per cent of starters they accounted for in 1997 to 20 per cent of starters by the end of 1999. The Family Income Supplement was reformed in 1998 to be calculated on the basis of net rather than gross income. The Back to Work Allowance and Area Based Enterprise Allowance have proved effective in ensuring that the transition from secure social welfare payments to insecure earnings did not entail a drop in living standards. The Local Employment Service was a major recommendation of the 1995 Task Force on Long-Term Unemployment and, by 1999, existed in eighteen particularly disadvantaged areas. Its purpose is 'to provide the gateway, or access point, to the full range of options which should be available to enable a long-term unemployed person return to the world of work'.

52. This is explicitly recognised in IBEC Dublin Regional Executive (1999), *Competitive Capital City: An Economic Strategy for Dublin.*

53. 'Justice while Unemployed' in *Work is the Key* (1992), paras. 121-128.

54. 'The increase in the returns to Junior Cert education between 1987 and 1994 … indicate a growth in demand for such workers. Preliminary data … for 1994-96 suggest that the average growth in hourly earnings for workers with Junior Cert qualifications was substantially higher than for any other education category' (Fitz Gerald *et al.,* 1999, p. 38).

55. Individual school principals, the Department of Education, IBEC and ICTU have all expressed their concern.

56. *Sharing in Progress: National Anti-Poverty Strategy* (1997), section 6.2.

57. Many people spoke to us of the concerns we write about here. In addition,

we acknowledge several written works that helped us to understand better and put in context what we were hearing. For example: B. Nolan, C. T. Whelan and J. Williams (1998), *Where Are Poor Households?;* J. Walsh, S. Craig and D. McCafferty (1998), *Local Partnerships for Social Inclusion?;* D.G. Pringle, J. Walsh and M. Hennessy (1999), *Poor People, Poor Places;* T. Fahey, ed. (1999), *Social Housing in Ireland;* B. Nolan and C. T. Whelan (1999), *Loading the Dice. A Study of Cumulative Disadvantage.*

58. Nolan *et al.* (1998).

59. The Health Research Board produces an annual national report on treated drug misuse in Ireland.

60. National Economic and Social Council (1981), *Urbanisation: Problems of Growth and Decay in Dublin.*

61. The 1996 Health Research Board report shows, for example, that, of all cases of treated drug misuse known to the National Drug Treatment System, 83 per cent were unemployed, 72 per cent were male, 65 per cent aged under 25, and 58 per cent had left school before the age of 15 (R. Moran, M. O'Brien and P. Duff, 1997).

62. There were twelve throughout the State by 1999.

63. Almost three quarters of the young men seeking treatment for drug abuse stated they were living with their parental family (1996).

64. During the preparation of this Letter, we were told there were approximately 3,000 treatment places nationally at a time when there were 13,000 known heroin users. Over 400 addicts were waiting for detoxification programmes in Dublin alone. Two pertinent publications from our 'Bishops' Initiative on Drug Use and Drug Addiction' are *Breaking the Silence* (1997) and *Tackling Drug Problems Together* (1998).

65. These values, however, are daily confronted with the behaviour of exceptionally disturbed and aggressive minorities, which can make their residents suffer twice over: they are the first victims of the anti-social behaviour of the minority in their midst, and the minority brings a stigma to where they live. See K. O'Higgins, 'Social Order Problems', and R. McAuliffe and T. Fahey, 'Responses to Social Order Problems' in Fahey, (1999).

66. The Community Employment and Community Development programmes, Area-Based Partnerships, URBAN, programmes for tackling educational disadvantage and the drugs menace, etc.

67. The Dublin Docklands Development Authority and the Integrated Area Plans of local authorities are prominent examples of attempts to adopt a holistic approach.

68. This importance to the economy of the overall quality of life available to knowledge-workers in Irish towns and cities was particularly emphasised by the ESRI and ICTU in their submissions on the National Development

Plan, 2000-2006. Tackling spatial concentrations of long-term unemployment and educational disadvantage is a principal concern of the Dublin Employment Pact on which many different groups have agreed. It also features strongly in IBEC Dublin Regional Executive (1999).

69. In some areas of Connemara, between 40 and 64 per cent of houses are holiday or second homes, their prices far in excess of what local people can afford; this problem is also significant in Leitrim. Where a large proportion of the local housing stock consists of holiday homes it means, not only that young local people cannot afford to buy a home in their own area, but that depopulation is given a further push, with the viability of local services of every sort being undermined. This has made some community organisations foresee 'collections of houses rather than a thriving community', and the development of 'a caretaker and lock-up society'.

70. There is a sense in which the factors bringing about the economic boom were quite secondary to an independent set of totally external factors dominating the fortunes of farmers – the momentum in global negotiations (WTO) towards free trade in agriculture, the restructuring of the EU's Common Agricultural Policy, the vicissitudes of weather, and arbitrary swings on international markets (effects of public health alarms, instability in the Middle East, etc.). In this sense, the farming community is on a different 'cycle' to that of the rest of the economy and correspondingly capable of being little understood or sympathised with.

71. A reflection by a group with a long experience of life in all its aspects in the West of Ireland, particularly of the lives of people who are socially marginalised in those counties, concludes: 'The present laudatory assessments of the positive impact of the Irish economy's success are, to a considerable extent, false'. See S. Airey (1999), *Challenging Voices: Pathways to Change. A Study of Justice and Spirituality by the Sisters of Mercy, Western Province.*

72. They faced an almost 22 per cent chance of being poor, as against 19 per cent for households in Dublin city and county. For this and the previous figures, see Nolan *et al.* (1998).

73. For the geographical distribution of educational disadvantage see T. Kellaghan, S. Weir, S. Ó hUallacháin and M. Morgan (1995), *Educational Disadvantage in Ireland.* The criteria for disadvantaged status make it almost impossible for rural schools in poor areas to qualify. Yet, for example, a recent survey of Co. Roscommon schools found that eleven had no teacher's toilet, twenty-five no staffroom, and twenty-one no hot water (address to INTO conference, 1999).

74. E. O'Shea (1996), 'Rural Poverty and Social Services Provision' in Curtin *et al.*

75. It has been observed that those organisations fare particularly well who

recognise and support in practical ways the transport costs arising from voluntary work. See P. O'Hara (1999), 'Partnerships and Rural Development', in Reynolds and Healy.

76. According to O'Hara (1999), those in farming occupations account for only a quarter of the rural labour force, while only half of household income on Irish farms comes from agriculture.

77. Between 1987 and 1995, largely because of the operation of the Common Agricultural Policy and reforms to it, large farms (over 100 hectares) saw average family farm income rise from £24,700 to £65,000, whereas the rise for the smallest farms was from £1,200 to £1,700 (from National Farm Surveys; see National Economic and Social Forum, 1997, *Rural Renewal – Combating Social Exclusion,* 2.11. Note: 'farm income' refers to earnings generated from farming only). For figures on the regressive distribution by farm size of direct payments specifically, see P. Commins (1996), 'Agricultural Production and Small-Scale Farming' in Curtin *et al.* (1996). *The Western People* (30 June 1999) reported on a fall of 8 per cent between 1992 and 1998 in the number of Co. Mayo farmers claiming livestock grants.

78. Organic producers are certified as meeting specific criteria in using sustainable management practices, avoiding damage to the environment and ensuring the ethical treatment of livestock.

79. This was the concern and central focus of the National Economic and Social Forum's report, *Rural Renewal – Combating Social Exclusion* (1997).

80. The internationally recognised achievements of Irish people with disabilities in literature, sport and European forums constitute so much evidence that their contributions in many areas of Irish life are being blocked by outdated attitudes, poorly designed buildings, and policies that have not been 'disability proofed'.

81. K. McKeown (1999), *Mentally Ill and Homeless in Ireland: Facing the Reality, Finding the Solutions.*

82. *A Strategy for Equality, Report of the Commission on the Status of People with Disabilities* (1996).

83. Pope John Paul II, *Laborem Exercens* (On Human Work), 14 September 1981.

84. *Report of the Committee of Inquiry into the Penal System* (1985).

85. 'One would have to go back to the early nineteenth century to find a time when prisons were as corrupting for those incarcerated in them': C. Lysaght (1998), 'Crime and Punishment' in K. Kennedy, ed., *From Famine to Feast: Economic and Social Change in Ireland, 1847-1997.*

86. Department of Justice (1997), *Report of Prison Service Operating Cost Review Group,* section 3.4.1.

87. P. O'Mahony (1997), *Mountjoy Prisoners: A Sociological and Criminological Profile.*

88. Both quotes are from Department of Justice (1994), *The Management of Offenders: A Five-Year Plan,* section 2.4.

89. Irish Episcopal Commission for Emigrants and Irish Commission for Prisoners Overseas (1999), *Emigration and Services for Irish Emigrants: Towards a New Strategic Plan:* section 7.2, 'Changing Understanding of the Nature of Emigration in Britain'.

90. There were approximately 5000 Traveller families at the end of the decade. They are a growing group within Irish society, their numbers estimated to increase by 26 per cent over the period 1995-2000. See *Report of the Task Force on the Travelling Community* (1995) for its population and accommodation projections to the year 2000. Earlier national reports were: *Report of the Commission on Itinerancy* (1963) and *Report of the Travelling People Review Body* (1983).

91. Department of the Environment and Local Government, 27 November 1998.

92. There are several encouraging examples of group housing and serviced sites which the Travelling People and local communities have found very satisfactory; see K. McKeown and B. McGrath (1996), *Accommodating Travelling People.*

93. Consult surveys by the Pilgrim House Community, Wexford, the Irish Refugee Council, Dublin, and the Irish Council for Overseas Students, Dublin. Also, Begley *et al.* (1999), *Asylum in Ireland: A Public Health Perspective.*

94. 'Accepting the Stranger into Our Community', Irish Catholic Bishops' Conference, Statement issued on 15 March 1999.

95. *Refugees and Asylum Seekers: A Challenge to Solidarity* (1997) A Joint Policy document of the Irish Commission for Justice and Peace and Trócaire.

96. Pope Paul VI, *Populorum Progressio* (The Development of Peoples), 26 March 1967.

97. 'Assessing Ireland's Infrastructure', Section 2.4 in Fitz Gerald *et al.* (1999).

98. See the sobering assessment of the lack of effective solidarity within 'one of the richest nations on earth' in *A Decade After Economic Justice for All* (1995), A Pastoral Message of the US National Conference of Catholic Bishops on the Tenth Anniversary of the Economic Pastoral.

99. The United Nations Development Programme now computes a human development index annually for each country. See also S. Healy and B. Reynolds, eds. (1996), *Progress, Values and Public Policy,* and K. E. Zappone and S. McNaughton (1999), 'Should We Stay at the Table (If There is One)? Evaluating Social Partnership in Ireland' in Reynolds and Healy.

100. These observations are based on data in Commission on the Family (1998), *Strengthening Families for Life,* Tables 2, A4a and A5a.

101. When single-parent households are added to twin-earner households, the

Annual Labour Force Survey 1997 suggests that a childminder or crèche is needed by more than one-half of Irish households if the parents are to work.

102. One written submission to us from a childminder was particularly poignant: 'Small children are wakened out of their sleep in the mornings and rushed out to their crèches or childminders. When they are collected in the evenings and brought home they cannot expect much attention from their parents as they both have to catch up with the cooking, cleaning, washing and shopping. Older children come home from school eager to tell their mother of all the day's happenings, but she is not there for them. As most homes now have more than one TV, they spend a lot of their time watching unsuitable programmes unsupervised'.

103. The number of people aged 80 and over in Ireland is set to rise substantially: specifically, by 17 per cent between 2001 and 2011; 20 per cent between 2011 and 2021; and 51 per cent between 2021 and 2031. See Central Statistics Office (1999), *Population and Labour Force Projections 2001-2031.*

104. Pope John Paul II, Address to the Elderly of Rome, 20 December 1987.

105. Pope John Paul II, *Dies Domini* (Keeping the Lord's Day Holy), 31 May 1998: 1, 67.

106. *Dies Domini,* 4.

107. The American economist, John Kenneth Galbraith, was invited to comment on what he thought, forty years after writing *The Affluent Society* (1958). He believed he had been insufficiently aware of a deep part of human nature which makes fortunate individuals and fortunate countries want to enjoy their wellbeing without the burden of conscience and without a troublesome sense of responsibility (*Human Development Report 1998,* p. 42).

108. Reich (1991) speaks of the 'secession' of the rich from American society: 'As the economic fates of Americans diverge, the top fifth may be losing the long-held sense of connectedness with the bottom fifth, or even the bottom four fifths…'. They are 'quietly seceding from the large and diverse publics of America into homogenous enclaves.' (p. 250 and p. 268.)

109. *The Work of Justice* (1977) observed that 'the areas where rich people live can be called ghettos too', para. 38.

110. *The Work of Justice* (1977), para. 36.

111. For example, the financial terms being insisted on in servicing their foreign debts.

112. At the end of the Berlin summit (26 March 1999), the Taoiseach, Bertie Ahern, TD, commented: 'Whoever is here in 2006 is very likely to be on the side I was fighting for the last two days – the net contributors'. For example, Ireland, with GNP per capita at 87 per cent of EU average, will

certainly be above the 90 per cent qualifying threshold for the Cohesion Fund by 2003.

113. It will take huge effort to ensure that an increased flow of funds is matched by no slippage in the quality of the uses to which they are put. Ireland's Official Development Assistance grew rapidly during the 1990s to reach 0.35 per cent of GNP in 1999, and received fulsome praise from the OECD for the quality of the programmes it was funding.

114. *Work is the Key* (1992), para. 120.

115. For example, the economy's future growth path would be directly affected by a large correction to share prices on the New York Stock Exchange, something that several commentators believe is inevitable: 'When does the Irish economic bubble burst? When will the US stock market collapse? … the two questions are so closely related that they are nearly the same. … the Irish economy has become a warrant on the US economy, with its massive growth most influenced by the direct foreign investment of leading US multinationals in this country…'. *Business & Finance*, 6 May 1999.

116. Pope John Paul II, *Redemptor Hominis* (Redeemer of Man), 6 March 1979. See also *Centesimus Annus*, 53.

117. Pope John Paul II, address in Puebla, Mexico, 1979 (*John Paul II in Mexico: His Collected Speeches*, 1979).

118. United Nations Development Programme (UNDP), 1998, p. 38.

119. A 1995 survey showed that Irish 11- to 17-year-olds, together with their English and Danish counterparts, drink more than teenagers in twenty-five other European countries. The topic of alcohol in Irish society was highlighted in a statement of the Irish Catholic Bishops' Conference, *The Temperate Way* (1999).

120. 'The aim (of the National Alcohol Policy) is to influence people's attitudes and habits so that, for those who choose to drink, moderate drinking becomes personally and socially acceptable and favoured in the Irish culture.' Department of Health (1996), *National Alcohol Policy*, p. 59.

121. *Work is the Key* (1992), paras. 47-60.

122. See Irish Episcopal Commission for Emigrants and Irish Commission for Prisoners Overseas (1999).

123. 'Only those who can be sure of solidarity from society as a whole, and are hence effectively protected against elementary risks, are willing to take on risks and to approve of the economic order in which they live.' (*Fairer Participation*, Memorandum of a Group of Experts working for the German Bishops' Conference for Societal and Social Matters, October 1998.)

124. By 1998, the number of births outside marriage had reached 28 per cent of all births in Ireland. Not all these children grow up without two parents, but the growth in one-parent families is also sobering: as a percentage of all

families with children under 15 years of age, they were 18 per cent in the 1996 Census (up from 11 per cent in 1991 and 7 per cent in 1981).

125. Such facts, and many others, are in Commission on the Family (1998). The Commission had special tabulations carried out on the 1996 Labour Force Survey. Some of the findings were: fathers work longer hours than men who are not fathers; 81 per cent of fathers with young children are in full-time jobs as against 55 per cent of men who are not fathers; 42 per cent of mothers with young children are in employment as against 24 per cent of women with older children; two out of every three mothers with young children in employment work full-time; and younger familes are twice as likely to have two earners (39 per cent) compared to older families.

126. The demand for childcare places is expected to increase by 50 per cent over the next ten years. Already, 'the lack of provision of quality childcare has reached a crisis level' (*National Childcare Strategy*, 1999), p. 10.

127. K. McKeown, H. Ferguson and D. Rooney (1998), *Changing Fathers? Fatherhood and Family Life in Modern Ireland.*

128. In addition to the Commission on the Family (1998), other important studies of the developing crisis in childcare are the *Report on the National Forum for Early Childhood Education to the Minister for Education and Science* (1998), and the *National Childcare Strategy: Report of the Partnership 2000 Expert Working Group on Childcare* (1999).

129. In 1997, 54.9 per cent of all Dutch women aged between 15 and 64 were in employment, but 67.9 per cent of them worked part-time; the corresponding figures for Dutch males were 78.1 per cent and 17.0 per cent. In Ireland, 45.3 per cent of all 15-64 year-old women were in employment, of whom 23.2 per cent worked part-time; the corresponding figures for Irish males were 70.2 per cent and 5.4 per cent. See European Commission (1998), *Employment In Europe 1998.*

130. 'Families and Work', Commission on the Family (1998), chapter 8.

131. Specifically, by 17 per cent between 2001 and 2011; 20 per cent between 2011 and 2021; and 51 per cent between 2021 and 2031. See Central Statistics Office (1999).

132. As the 1990s ended, there was not a reliable picture of developments in earnings inequality over the second half of the decade. Irish society should await the evidence with great interest and deep concern. The gap had widened between 1987 and 1994: in a comparison of fourteen industrial countries, Ireland recorded the largest deterioration in earnings inequality over the period. It is also known that the proportion of full-time employees who were low-paid rose from 21 per cent to 24 per cent (see Barrett *et al.*, 1999). Since 1994, the picture is less clear. Young, well-educated people who joined the workforce, or returned to it from overseas have been able to progress more quickly to good levels of earnings thanks to their better

opportunities. As 1999 ended, it was not clear to what extent the announcement of a statutory minimim wage and, above all, the beneficial effects of competition in bidding up what employers have had to offer at the bottom of the labour ladder, have improved the relative earnings of older workers with little formal education.

133. The Irish National Organisation of the Unemployed make the proposal for a targeted 'job guarantee' in this way: 'Every person who has been unemployed for five years or more should be invited for interview by the Local Employment Service or FÁS. Attendance at the interview should be voluntary. The interview would explore the range of training and education programmes available. Also on offer would be the guarantee of an ongoing job in the social economy at the going rate. Sufficient meaningful jobs at the appropriate skills level would be created to guarantee such employment to all those over five years unemployed who took up the option.'

134. Irish Congress of Trade Unions (1997), *Five Pounds an Hour: The Case for a Fair Minimum Wage,* submission to Minimum Wage Commission, p. 4.

135. *The Work of Justice* (1997), para. 72.

136. Though rejected by the 1996 *Report of the Constitution Review Group,* the Irish Commission for Justice and Peace, a Commission of the Bishops' Conference, has put forward cogent arguments for the inclusion of these rights in the Constitution. See Irish Commission for Justice and Peace (1998), *Re-Righting the Constitution: The Case for New Social and Economic Rights: Housing, Health, Nutrition, Adequate Standard of Living.*

137. See, for example, M. MacFarlan and H. Oxley (1996), 'Social Transfers: Spending Patterns, Institutional Arrangements and Policy Responses', *OECD Economic Studies,* No. 27, 1996/II.

138. The Pensions Board (1998), *Securing Retirement Income,* p. 87. It adopted this figure for reasons of 'practicality' and acknowledged this was still at the lower end of the norm in EU countries. There is need for a much wider debate on whether this 34 per cent figure is satisfactory.

139. The total valid poll in General Elections between 1981 and 1997 is as follows (expressed as a percentage of the electorate): 75.5 per cent (1981), 73.2 per cent (February 1982), 72.3 per cent (November 1982), 72.7 per cent (1987), 67.7 per cent (1989), 67.5 per cent (1992), 65.3 per cent (1997). We commend the important work of the Vincentian Partnership for Justice in seeking to raise awareness and electoral participation in disadvantaged communities.

140. Results of a national survey conducted for the Irish Congress of Trade Unions, ICTU (1998), *What People Think of Unions.*

I. CHURCH DOCUMENTS

a.   Papal and Vatican Documents

POPE JOHN XXIII, *Pacem in Terris* (Peace on Earth), 11 April 1963, London: Catholic Truth Society.

POPE PAUL VI, *Populorum Progressio* (The Development of Peoples), 26 March 1967, London: Catholic Truth Society.

POPE JOHN PAUL II, *Redemptor Hominis* (Redeemer of Man), 4 March 1979, London: Catholic Truth Society.

POPE JOHN PAUL II, *Laborem Exercens* (On Human Work), 14 September 1981, London: Catholic Truth Society.

POPE JOHN PAUL II, *Sollicitudo Rei Socialis* (The Social Concern of the Church), 30 December 1987, London: Catholic Truth Society.

POPE JOHN PAUL II, *Centesimus Annus* (The Hundredth Anniversary), 1 May 1991, London: Catholic Truth Society.

POPE JOHN PAUL II, *Tertio Millennio Adveniente* (Preparation for the Jubilee of the Year 2000), 10 November 1994, London: Catholic Truth Society.

POPE JOHN PAUL II, *Dies Domini* (Keeping the Lord's Day Holy), 31 May 1998, Dublin: Veritas.

VATICAN II, *Gaudium et Spes (Pastoral Constitution on the Church in the Modern World)*, 7 December 1965 in A. Flannery OP, general editor (1996), *Vatican Council II: Constitutions, Decrees, Declarations,* Dublin: Dominican Publications.

John Paul II in Mexico: His Collected Speeches (1979), London: Collins.

b.   Other Texts

Christian Faith in a Time of Economic Depression, A Statement from the Irish Episcopal Conference at its General Meeting, 15 June 1983.

The Common Good and the Catholic Church's Social Teaching (1996), A Statement by the Catholic Bishops' Conference of England & Wales, London: The Catholic Bishops' Conference of England & Wales.

THE IRISH CATHOLIC BISHOPS' CONFERENCE, (1999), *The Temperate Way.*

IRISH CATHOLIC BISHOPS' CONFERENCE, *Accepting the Stranger into our Community, Statement,* 15 March 1999.

IRISH EPISCOPAL CONFERENCE (1992), *Work is the Key: Towards an Economy that Needs Everyone,* Dublin: Veritas.

The Work of Justice, Irish Bishops' Pastoral (1977), Dublin: Veritas.

US NATIONAL CONFERENCE OF CATHOLIC BISHOPS (1995), A Decade After Economic Justice for All, A Pastoral Message on the Tenth Anniversary of the Economic Pastoral, Washington DC: United States Catholic Conference.

II. ECONOMIC AND SOCIAL SOURCES CITED

AIREY, S. (1999), *Challenging Voices: Pathways to Change*, A Study of Justice and Spirituality by the Sisters of Mercy, Western Province, Ballinasloe: Sisters of Mercy, Western Province.

ALLEN, M. (1998), *The Bitter Word: Ireland's Job Famine and its Aftermath*, Dublin: Poolbeg Press.

BACON, P. & Associates (1998), *An Economic Assessment of Recent House Price Developments*, Dublin: Stationery Office.

BACON, P. & Associates (1999), *The Housing Market: An Economic Review and Assessment*, Dublin: Stationery Office.

BARRETT, A., T. CALLAN and B. NOLAN (1999), 'Rising Wage Inequality, Returns to Education and Labour Market Institutions: Evidence from Ireland', *British Journal of Industrial Relations*, 37:1.

BARRY, F. ed. (1999), *Understanding Ireland's Economic Growth*, London: Macmillan.

BEGLEY, M. *et al.* (1999), *Asylum in Ireland: A Public Health Perspective*, Dublin: Department of Public Health Medicine and Epidemiology, University College Dublin in association with Congregation of the Holy Ghost, Dublin.

BRADLEY, J., J. FITZGERALD, P. HONOHAN and I. KEARNEY (1997), 'Interpreting the Recent Irish Growth Experience' in D. Duffy, J. FitzGerald, I. Kearney and F. Shorthall, eds., *Medium Term Review: 1997-2003*, Dublin: ESRI.

CALLAN, T. *et al.* (1999), *Monitoring Trends in Poverty for the National Anti-Poverty Strategy*, Final Report, Dublin: ESRI.

CENTRAL STATISTICS OFFICE (1999), *Population and Labour Force Projections 2001-2031*, Dublin: Stationery Office.

COMMINS, P. (1996), 'Agricultural Production and Small-Scale Farming' in C. Curtin, T. Hasse and H. Tovey, eds., *Poverty in Rural Ireland: A Political Economy Perspective*, Dublin: Oak Tree Press.

COMMISSION ON THE FAMILY (1998), *Strengthening Families for Life*, Dublin: Stationery Office.

CURTIN, C., T. HAASE and H. TOVEY, eds. (1996), *Poverty in Rural Ireland: A Political Economy Perspective*, Dublin: Oak Tree Press.

DEPARTMENT OF THE ENVIRONMENT AND LOCAL GOVERNMENT (1997), *Sustainable Development: A Strategy for Ireland,* Dublin: Stationery Office.

DEPARTMENT OF THE ENVIRONMENT AND LOCAL GOVERNMENT (1999), *Annual Housing Statistics Bulletin 1998,* Dublin: Stationery Office.

DEPARTMENT OF HEALTH (1996), *National Alcohol Policy,* Dublin: Stationery Office.

DEPARTMENT OF JUSTICE (1994), *The Management of Offenders: A Five Year Plan,* Dublin: Stationery Office.

DEPARTMENT OF JUSTICE (1997), *Report of Prison Service Operating Cost Review Group,* Dublin: Stationery Office.

EUROPEAN COMMISSION (1998), *Employment in Europe 1998,* Brussels: Directorate-General for Employment, Industrial Relations and Social Affairs.

EUROPEAN SOCIAL FUND PROGRAMME EVALUATION UNIT (1998), *ESF and the Long Term Unemployed,* Dublin: European Social Fund Programme Evaluation Unit, Department of Enterprise and Employment.

FAHEY, T., ed. (1999), *Social Housing in Ireland: A Study of Success, Failure and Lessons Learned,* Dublin: Oak Tree Press.

FITZGERALD, J., I. KEARNEY, E. MORGENROTH and D. SMYTH, eds. (1999), *National Investment Priorities for the Period 2000-2006,* Dublin: ESRI (Policy Research Series, No. 33).

GOTTSCHALK, P. and T. SMEEDING (1997), 'Cross-National Comparisons of Earnings and Income Inequality', *Journal of Economic Literature,* Vol. XXXV, June.

GRAY, A., ed. (1997), *International Perspectives on the Irish Economy,* Dublin: Indecon.

HARVEY, B. (1994), *Combating Exclusion: Lessons from the Third EU Poverty Programme in Ireland 1989-1994,* Dublin: Combat Poverty Agency.

HEALY, S. and B. REYNOLDS (1996), *Progress, Values and Public Policy,* Dublin: CORI Justice Commission.

IBEC DUBLIN REGIONAL EXECUTIVE (1999), *Competitive Capital City: An Economic Strategy for Dublin,* Dublin.

IRISH CONGRESS OF TRADE UNIONS (1997), *Five Pounds an Hour: The Case for a Fair Minimu Wage,* submission to Minimum Wage Commission, Dublin: ICTU.

IRISH CONGRESS OF TRADE UNIONS (1998), *What People Think of Unions,* Dublin: ICTU.

ILO (1999), *Social Dialogue and Employment Success: Europe's Employment Revival – Four Small European Countries Compared,* Geneva: ILO.

IRISH COMMISSION FOR JUSTICE AND PEACE (1998), *Re-Righting the Constitution – The Case for New Social and Economic Rights: Housing, Health, Nutrition, Adequate Standard of Living,* Dublin.

IRISH EPISCOPAL COMMISSION FOR EMIGRANTS and THE IRISH COMMISSION FOR PRISONERS OVERSEAS (1999), *Emigration and Services for Irish Emigrants: Towards a New Strategic Plan,* Dublin.

JACKSON, J. A. and T. HASSE (1996), 'Demography and the Distribution of Deprivation in Rural Ireland' in C. Curtin, T. Haase and H. Tovey, eds., *Poverty in Rural Ireland: A Political Economy Perspective,* Dublin: Oak Tree Press.

JOYCE, L. and A. McCASHIN, compilers (1981), *Poverty and Social Policy,* Dublin: Institute of Public Administration.

KELLEGHAN, T., S. WEIR, S. O'hUALLACHAIN and M. MORGAN (1995), *Educational Disadvantage in Ireland,* Dublin: Department of Education.

LYSAGHT, C. (1998), 'Crime and Punishment' in K. Kennedy, ed., *From Famine to Feast: Economic and Social Change in Ireland, 1847-1997,* Dublin: Institute of Public Administration.

MacFARLAN, M. and H. OXLEY (1996), 'Social Transfers: Spending Patterns, Institutional Arrangements and Policy Responses', *OECD Economic Studies,* No. 27, 1996/II.

McAULIFFE, R. and T. FAHEY (1999), 'Responses to Social Order Problems' in T. Fahey, ed., *Social Housing in Ireland: A Study of Success, Failure and Lessons Learned,* Dublin: Oak Tree Press.

McKEOWN, K. (1999), *Mentally Ill and Homeless in Ireland: Facing the Reality, Finding the Solutions,* Dublin: Disability Federation of Ireland.

McKEOWN, K. and B. McGRATH (1996), *Accommodating Travelling People,* Dublin: CROSSCARE.

McKEOWN, K., H. FERGUSON and H. ROONEY (1998), *Changing Fathers? Fatherhood and Family Life in Modern Ireland,* Dublin: The Collins Press.

McVERRY, P. (1999), 'Twenty-Five Years of Homelessness', *Working Notes,* Issue 35.

MARRIS, R. (1996), *How to Save the Underclass,* London: Macmillan Press.

MORAN, R., M. O'BRIEN and P. DUFF (1997), *Treated Drug Misuse in Ireland National Report 1996,* Dublin: Health Research Board.

National Childcare Strategy: Report of the Partnership 2000 Expert Working Group on Childcare (1999), Dublin: Stationery Office.

NATIONAL ECONOMIC AND SOCIAL COUNCIL (1981), *Urbanisation: Problems of Growth and Decay in Dublin,* Dublin: Stationery Office (NESC Report No. 55).

NATIONAL ECONOMIC AND SOCIAL FORUM (1997), *Rural Renewal – Combating Social Exclusion,* Dublin: National Economic and Social Forum.

NOLAN, B. and T. CALLAN (1994), *Poverty and Policy,* Dublin: Gill and Macmillan.

NOLAN, B., T. CALLAN, C. WHELAN and J. WILLIAMS (1994), *Poverty and Time: Perspectives on the Dynamics of Poverty,* Dublin: ESRI (General Research Series, No. 166).

NOLAN B. and C.T. WHELAN (1996), *Resources, Deprivation and Poverty,* Oxford: Clarendon Press.

NOLAN, B., C.T. WHELAN and J. WILLIAMS (1998), *Where Are Poor Households? The Spatial Distribution of Poverty and Deprivation in Ireland,* Dublin: Oak Tree Press.

NOLAN, B. and C.T. Whelan (1999), *Loading the Dice: A Study of Cumulative Disadvantage,* Dublin: Oak Tree Press.

NORTH, D.C. (1990), *Institutions, Institutional Change and Economic Performance,* Cambridge: Cambridge University Press.

OECD (1998), *OECD Economic Outlook,* December 1998, Paris: OECD.

OECD (1999), *OECD Economic Surveys,* 1998-1999: Ireland, Paris: OECD.

O'CONNELL, P. and F. McGINNITY (1997), *Working Schemes: Active Labour Market Policy in Ireland,* Dublin: Ashgate/ESRI.

O'HARA, P. (1999), 'Partnerships and Rural Development' in B. Reynolds and S. Healy, eds., *Social Partnership in a New Century,* Dublin: CORI Justice Commission.

O'HIGGINS, K. (1999), 'Social Order Problems' in T. Fahey, ed., *Social Housing in Ireland: A Study of Success, Failure and Lessons Learned,* Dublin: Oak Tree Press.

O'MAHONY, P. (1997), *Mountjoy Prisoners: A Sociological and Criminological Profile,* Dublin: Department of Justice.

O'SHEA, E. (1996), 'Rural Poverty and Social Services Provision' in C. Curtin, T. Haase and H. Tovey, eds., *Poverty in Rural Ireland: A Political Economy Perspective,* Dublin: Oak Tree Press.

THE PENSIONS BOARD (1998), *Securing Retirement Income: National Pensions Policy Initiative,* Report of the Pensions Board to the Minister for Social, Community and Family Affairs, Dublin: The Pensions Board.

PHELPS, E. S. (1997), *Rewarding Work: How to Restore Participation and Self-Support to Free Enterprise,* Cambridge, Mass: Harvard University Press.

PLATTEAU, J. P. (1994), 'Behind the Market Stage Where Real Societies Exist', *Journal of Development Studies,* Vol. 30, Parts I and II.

PRINGLE, D. G., J. WALSH and M. HENNESSY (1999), *Poor People, Poor Places,* Dublin: Oak Tree Press.

Programme for National Recovery (1987), Dublin: Stationery Office.

Programme for Economic and Social Progress (1991), Dublin: Stationery Office.

Programme for Competitiveness and Work (1994), Dublin: Stationery Office.

Partnership 2000 for Inclusion, Employment and Competitiveness (1996), Dublin: Stationery Office.

PUTNAM, R.D., R. LEONARDI and R.Y. NANETT (1994), *Making Democracy Work: Civic Traditions in Modern Italy*, Princeton, N.J.: Princeton University Press.

REICH, R.B. (1991), *The Work of Nations: Preparing Ourselves for 21st Century Capitalism*, New York: Knopf Inc.

Refugees and Asylum Seekers: A Challenge to Solidarity (1997), A Joint Policy Document of the Irish Commission for Justice & Peace and Trócaire, Dublin.

Report of the Committee of Inquiry Into the Penal System (1985), Dublin: Stationery Office.

Report of the Task Force on the Travelling Community (1995), Dublin: Stationery Office.

REYNOLDS, B. and S. HEALY, eds. (1999), *Social Partnership in a New Century*, Dublin: CORI Justice Commission.

Sharing in Progress: National Anti-Poverty Strategy, (1997), Dublin: Stationery Office.

Social Studies, Vol. 1, No. 4, August 1972.

SOCIETY OF SAINT VINCENT DE PAUL (1999), *Housing Policy: Mixed Housing and Mixed Communities,* Dublin: Society of Saint Vincent de Paul.

A Strategy for Equality (1996), Report of the Commission on the Status of People with Disabilities, Dublin: Stationery Office.

TANSEY, P. (1998), *Ireland at Work: Economic Growth and the Labour Market,* Dublin: Oak Tree Press.

UNITED NATIONS DEVELOPMENT PROGRAMME (1998), *Human Development Report 1998,* Oxford: Oxford University Press.

WALSH, J., S. CRAIG and D. McCAFFERTY (1998), *Local Partnerships for Social Inclusion?,* Dublin: Oak Tree Press.

WILLIAMS, J. and M. O'CONNOR (1999), *Counted In: The Report of the 1999 Assessment of Homelessness in Dublin, Kildare and Wicklow,* Dublin: Homeless Initiative.

ZAPPONE, K.E. and S. McNAUGHTON (1999), 'Should We Stay at the Table (If There is One?), Evaluating Social Partnership in Ireland' in B. Reynolds and S. Healy, eds., *Social Partnership in a New Century,* Dublin: CORI Justice Commission.